The ALPHA BOATS ODYSSEY

The ALPHA BOATS ODYSSEY

A True Sea Story to Remember

ROBERT E. MURRAY

Advantage™

Published by Advantage, Charleston, South Carolina.
Member of Advantage Media Group.

Printed in the United States of America

ISBN: 978-1-59932-020-5

Cover photograph by Jimmy White. Top left to right: Walt, Rick; Bottom: Bob, Dan.

foreword

Charley Willis asked Bob: "Why don't you take one of the boats to Ghana? You could take your boys as crew. It would be a trip they would never forget."

Yes, he thought, the boys were very good students and athletically inclined, but they did need something to hang their hats on, and missed opportunities was not one of them. Here was opportunity handed on a silver platter, with one very special benefit. It's called bonding. Certainly he would go, provided the boys accepted the challenge. In the experience would be lessons in source management, planning, navigation, and discipline that normally they could only get the textbook version of at school. Yes, it could bring with it far-reaching effects as far as individual development was concerned!

Bob answered, "We'll do it, providing that the boys are willing and we can convince their mother that it's best for them. I'm sure the boys will be gung ho, but I think we'll have to do a sales job on their mother. The IRS thing is still looming over our heads and if this offers an avenue of relief, I don't think that should be too difficult."

How often do we pass on solid opportunities for the practical applications of life's lessons because of the fear of failure? That fear can be real. After raising a child for fifteen or twenty years, any parent may be reluctant to push them out onto the street prematurely if there is a better means of preparation. And there is!

When we accept the privilege of raising children, we also accept the responsibilities of helping to develop their character.

It's called "bonding, – i.e, to connect with. Here was a perfect opportunity for Bob to *bond* with his sons." But he must remember they were Jo's sons as well! When Bob was with Alaska Airlines, there were many opportunities that opened up, but none as strong as this one promised to be. He took them to Alaska several times, just the two older boys, where they panned for gold in Nome, watched ivory carvers as they plied their craft, experienced blanket tosses with the Eskimos in Kotzebue, explored the gold dredges in Fairbanks, and chatted with many of the elder aviation pioneers throughout the state. Men like Jim Magoffin of Interior Airways, Bob Reeves of Reeves Aleutian Airways, Lanky Rice of Northern Consolidated Airlines, and the Wein boys of Wein Airlines - not to mention Charley Willis.

To understand the background and setting of this account, one must first ask: Who was Cmdr. Charles F. Willis, U S Navy, ret.?
Cmdr. Charles Fountain Willis, Jr., was a highly decorated Naval Aviator during WW2 with twenty-three major citations and decorations. Charley served three tours of duty in WW II and was awarded twenty-three major medals and commendations including the Purple Heart, three Distinguished Flying Crosses, and three Air Medals during WW II. He co-founded "Citizens for Eisenhower" during Eisenhower's successful run for the presidency in 1948. Willis is credited with coining the phrase, "I like Ike." After the election, he served as a Special Assistant to the President on Aviation Matters, and was appointed Finance Chairman and National Chairman for the US Committee for the United Nations. Later in 1956, he was appointed President, Chairman, and Chief Executive Officer of Alaska Airlines, Inc, when that company had serious problems with its current management and was in danger of losing its postal subsidy program (a federal program whereby many economically or transportation challenged communities were supported in part by the federal government providing a mail subsidy to those carriers serving areas relatively inaccessible by normal delivery methods). Alaska fell within the bounds of this regulation because of its lack of roads. The state was served principally by air. Such a program was considered essential at that time to the survival of communications contacts throughout Alaska. (At that time, Alaska Airlines survival was dependent on the mail subsidy income, as were the economies of the towns and villages north of the Artic Circle to have their contact with the "lower forty-eight" maintained.)

Robert E. Murray joined Alaska Airlines in January, 1961, from Boeing's B-52 training program, and after a short tenure was appointed the company's first Director of Training, a new junior management position to keep pace with developments within he airline industry as a whole. He held this position for three years and was then promoted to Administrative Assistant to the President, both where he traveled extensively to settle company problem areas domestically and overseas. He was elected by the membership of the Air Transport Association to represent the eight Alaskan Carriers in the upcoming negotiations with the Federal Aviation Administration regarding the newly promulgated Training Regulations affecting all US carriers. He was a co-founder with Mr. Willis of National Aviation Academy in St. Petersburg, Florida, and was its first President. As President of NAA, Robert Murray was instrumental in developing an integrated training program permitting an applicant with no previous flight experience to graduate in 160 hours of flight time, with both a commercial pilot's license and an instrument rating, as well as a multi-engine rating. At the time, pilots were required to have 200 hours of flight time before they could be considered for the commercial pilot's certificate. This program became the standard against which flight schools were evaluated. At NAA, Bob Murray also employed Charley Willis' 30-foot twin screw cabin cruiser named the Sea Esta to entertain officials from major carriers from around the country who came to address the aspiring aviators - speakers such as Dave Garrett, VP, and later president of Delta Airlines, Capt. Spence Marsh, Director of Training for Northwest, and others of similar caliber, speakers from Frontier, Eastern, Braniff, Ozark, Pan American, National, and United Air Lines.

Thanks go to Jimmy White, to the Murray boys - Rick, Dan, and Walt - as well as the spouses involved whose infallible memories helped insure the accuracy of this chronicle. To Ben Toy and Alice Crogan of Advantage Media Group for their dogged determination in bringing this work to print – ***many thanks also to Ann Summer of Advantage for her editing of this work, as well as David Welday in structuring the marketing effort***

chapter one

PROSPECTING

It was a small, insignificant article in the *New York Herald Tribune* International Edition. Charley's eye skimmed over it and he was about to turn the page when a mental alarm went off. That alarm had spelled *opportunity* in the past. Africa had been good hunting ground for opportunity, particularly for someone with Charley Willis' experience and contacts in international politics ... and his intuition. Opportunities for Charley usually came from insider information and permitted him to go to the front of the line. He normally paid little attention to those items that lasted long enough to make it to the interior pages of the newspaper. If a good opportunity lasted that long, it was usually wire-bound and gagged by multiple levels of politicians and the ranking military. As he re-read the article, however, the feeling came over him that this might be different:

> The government of Ghana announced today that it had renewed its contract with Senegalese interests to fish Ghanaian waters. Under the contract, the catch would be the property of the government of Ghana for resale and distribution to feed its people through authorized seafood distributors. The operation, based at the seaport of Tema, last year produced over twenty thousand tons of fish at a cost of thirty seven million Cedis....

The article went on to quote the Minister of Agriculture and others - both in and out of government - but Charley was busy turning those figures around in his head. *Why are they contracting for others to fish their waters for them? Why?* he wondered.

Then it dawned on him. The major fishing effort locally was done by literally hundreds of open canoes with capacities of only a few hundred pounds each. They fished close to shore in the early morning and were usually finished before noon. They took their catch to market in the afternoon. All their catch was sold in local markets, and very little ever made it to the interior villages. These boats did very well for the owner and three-man crew, but to feed a nation of 15 million people? The more Charley thought about it, the more reasonable it seemed for Ghana to set up their own fishing fleet. After all, thirty seven million Cedis is a lot of money! Over twenty million dollars!

He thumped the article with his finger and said aloud, "Yes, this could be what I've come to Africa for!" Embarrassed, he glanced around to see if anyone was listening to him talking to himself. Relieved that no one appeared to be paying attention to him, he read the article again. A plan began to take shape.

It didn't seem strange to him that he was not noticed. He learned long ago that the center of attention doesn't gather information except in a meeting called for that purpose. He didn't want to draw attention to himself - at least not at this point. He mumbled something about keeping his ears open and his mouth shut and continued his reading, the skeleton of opportunity again rising from the shadows of his mind. He would need to find at least a couple of boats, preferably of the same manufacturer, to keep their spares program simple. They would have to be crewed. And they would need fuel. But fuel! That could be arranged right here in Accra by the boys at Texaco. Charley had a good relationship with Texaco, dating back several years thru Don Mulkey when Charley had airplanes moving in and out of Accra on a rather regular basis. Don was no longer in New York, but had been transferred to Houston when Texaco moved their "Head Shed" from New York to Houston in the middle sixties.

There was nothing unusual about him except, perhaps, his height. While he was seated, at six foot one, he did stand taller than most in Accra. His face was his only notable feature, and that only if a sculptor in search of a subject happened by. His mouth, framed by two deep ravines extending from his nose downward, commanded the lower face. The sharply carved features overruled the sagging jowls that gave evidence of oncoming old age, or of excesses in the party circuit. In Charley's case, it was a tossup. At sixty-one, his athletic build was still very apparent. A competition swimmer in college, he had been careful to maintain a degree of fitness that many of his generation would now be willing to pay dearly for. His face, however, was like a road map –
well worn and etched with emotions.

Recent trials seem to etch themselves indelibly in the furrowed brow and the two exclamatory indentations between the dark eyebrows. The loss of his wife three years ago to divorce left the deepest mark, both inwardly and on the surface, but his remarriage last year had helped to stabilize him ... except that Victoria (Vi for short) was not his constant companion on these prospecting ventures. The major difference between the two was that Vi did not like to travel.

His middle years were happy ones, filled with business successes visits to many foreign lands and children who had not yet discovered the addictive habits that leave hollow shells. Crinkles at his eyes remained as evidence of memories eager to be shared. The fact that these characteristics were deep and indelible indicated Charley's intensity for any undertaking. Over the years, these dedicated purposes had been an inspiration to many who had worked with (and for) him, resulting in outward appearances far beyond what nature had intended.

Charley was no neophyte in maneuvering in the inner circles of power. His first step was always to decide who held that power. Governments are notoriously populated with figureheads, but the string-pullers - that's who Charley needed to identify. Then, ally himself with one who has undisputed access to the string-puller, or to the string-puller himself. And stay in the background! The shadow image was important and required careful grooming. In foreign lands, it was important to appear as a string-puller in your own time and place, because those in power recognize such a person as one of the clan. Success in this game was not for the weak of heart!

First, he should go to Tema. Get a handle on the fishing operation. Who controlled the docks, not the bureaucratic control administered by political empire builders but the back street behind-the-scenes power that ultimately determined who was to profit from the enterprise and by how much. He needed to know where the fishing grounds were, how prolific they were, and what they produced. *No,* he thought, *that's secondary. That's production. The first goal is to get the gravy train on track, and get a head of steam in the boiler!*

Charley had been to Tema before. It had always been a pleasant half-hour drive from Accra, whether by the Autoroute or by the seashore. This time, however, he was oblivious to the passing scenery. He sifted through the numbers again and again, each time coming back to a two-boat program.

Not that two mid-sized fishing trawlers would replace the Senegalese - they would not, nor would he want them to. To propose an untried concept replacing, in toto, a proven, successful program did not make sense to Charley, and he was certain that it would not make sense to the Ghanaians. No, the idea would be to sell the concept of self-determination, of self-sufficiency. That could be an easy sale, easier too, to monitor and expand. Yes, two, maybe three boats are all he would need to set up his long-term annuity. He could probably realize $50,000 plus a few "benny points" along the way, or even more for putting the deal together. And if it was successful, there was literally no limit to what it could mean. *Thirty seven million Cedi's a year! Not a bad operating budget!*

Thirty-seven million in Cedis. Let's see, that's more than twelve million, that's over twenty million dollars!

"Excuse me?" the driver said.

"What was that?" Charley replied.

"I thought you said something to me, Sir."

"No, Toluto, I was just talking to myself. Drive down the dock and park in front of the Port Authority offices. I just want to sit in the car for a few minutes before I go inside."

chapter two

THE TEMA PORT DOCKS

Toluto acknowledged Charley, but he parked so Charley's view of the dock was partially obscured. Charley decided not to have him move the car. He decided to walk down the dock instead.

"I'm going to walk a bit. Wait for me here. We'll go back to Accra in about an hour."

"Yes sir, Mr. Willis, I'll be right here."

As he stepped out of the car, an old acquaintance and former partner in their air freight operation, Bertram Amin, came out of the Port Authority. Instantly Charley's caution flags were hoisted, for Bert had a similar sixth sense regarding opportunities. But he didn't discount the fact that they had made good money together in the past. As he greeted Bertram, Charley wondered if they were both there for the same purpose. Even so, here was one man who had opened any door in government a few years earlier when Charley was operating cargo DC-8s into Africa.

"Hey, Bert, good to see you. I didn't know you ran the port dock, too!"

"Charley! Where did you come from? What are you doing here? Hey, man, we gotta talk! Where you going? You come to see old Bert? How did you know I was here?"

"Whoa! Hold it! One question at a time!" Charley laughed. "I came in from the States yesterday, just trolling around looking for a way to make a buck."

"Hey, man, don't feed me that crap. You don't go to the bathroom without a reason! Now, what brings you back to Ghana?"

"Actually, I was headed for Nigeria - I was told about some things going on there, some business we may be interested in. A friend in Washington just came back from Lagos. He told me about trying to catch a local commuter flight. It sounded like something out of a Keystone Cops comedy. Oh well, you wouldn't know about that, but just say it was a comedy of errors."

"What's that?"

"John was waiting to catch a flight from Kanos to Lagos on a local charter – I guess you'd call it an airline. The plane had nineteen or twenty seats, and he guessed there were at least fifty people waiting for the plane to arrive. Everyone had a ticket. When the plane did arrive, there were four people escorted to the plane. John guessed they were the "First Class" passengers because they were assured a seat. When these were on board, the gate agent came back and opened the gate. All fifty people tried to squeeze through that three-foot gate at the same time. The first fifteen or sixteen got on board and the rest just ambled back to the gate to wait for the next airplane. They were so nonchalant about it that John figured only way to be sure he made the next flight was to go First Class. He slipped the gate agent a hundred Naira's and was the first one on board. John's story was longer and funnier because he experienced the total organized confusion and it was still vivid in his mind. But I figured any place that operates with a 250% load factor has to have some profit in the picture somewhere. I couldn't get a seat into Lagos from New York, so I decided to stop off and see what's gong on here in Happy Land."

Bertram's smile didn't fade. He asked, "But what are you doing *here*? Airplanes don't land at Tema. Have you found a sack of diamonds? What's happening?"

"Wait a minute! It's your turn to answer one. I thought Accra was your playground. What brings you to Tema?"

Bertram's lack of hesitation assured Charley that his response was open, perhaps even true. "A friend of mine has a business on the docks, and I do a little work for her - you know, government offices and all that."

Bertram's eyes narrowed slightly, as if contemplating. "Listen, how long will you be here? I mean, you stopped off here looking for something. If you found something, how long would you stay? Where are you staying? And when you came in yesterday, why didn't you call me?" Then he laughed, "I know, I know. I'm asking all these machine gun questions again. But we've got a lot to talk about, so what's your schedule? When can we get together?"

"I'm going to be here a couple more days, and I can stop back after Lagos next week if there's something to stop for. I'm at the KLM. Why don't we get together for dinner tonight?"

"Eight o'clock?", Bertram asked.

"Is the Majararaja still open? They used to have excellent curry dishes."
"Deal! I'll call the domo for two at eight."

"Great!"

As he watched Bertram walk away, Charley smiled at the same old arrogant stride that exuded confidence, some of it well taken. Bert was not tall - a stocky 5' 6 or 7 - the two of them made a fair replica of Mutt and Jeff, without the mustache. Bert looked like a welder or pipe fitter turned politician. He wore his white shirt and tie like a badge of honor, marking him as one above menial labor and therefore a person to be respected. It was true that others tried to gain respect by their dress codes, but without access to the seats of power, their attempts were usually short lived. They would be soon found back on the labor scene holding only the satisfaction of knowing they had tried. They were one of the boys again. Bert was different. He was one of the boys, but one with authority. He could work both sides of the street, a bit of knowledge firmly implanted in Charley's mind by reason of experience.

Charley got that familiar feeling that this was another work of Providence. But before he confided in Bertram, he would have to know more, a lot more, about him - who he was currently associating with, and what promises was he working on that he hadn't broken yet. A lot of changes can take place in three years. In his past dealing with Bert, Charley controlled the business and had the knowledge to go with it. This was a different time, a different set of circumstances. Different enough to warrant caution. With all they had been through together, he easily could have leaned on his prior evaluation of Bertram. Today, however, Bertram was just another blank canvas waiting for the brush.

The dock scene was typical of docks the world over, and tropical docks in particular. Gasoline and diesel fumes mixed randomly with the odor of rotting fruits and vegetables spiced by decaying fish. Occasionally an offshore breeze parted the evidence of human carelessness in the name of enterprise, and all but the hardcore dockhand lifted their heads to capture what they could of Nature's most welcome blessing. Charley was no exception. It was then he realized how the docks could dull those senses most offended. The breeze, as brief a respite as it was, put this little part of the world back into perspective. He could see how men could work during the day, but how could they get started in the morning? Perhaps it wasn't so bad in the early hours, before the mass of people, before the screech and roar of the machinery, before the oppressive heat, and before organic refuse littered the dock.

That was probably the answer. Garbage! As Charley watched the vendors husking and topping coconuts, slicing and serving fresh pineapple and customers pitching banana peels at random, he began to appreciate the magnitude of the problem. In the course of the day, it grew to substantial proportions, aided in its decay by the ever-present sun. And the process was renewed each morning! He later learned that they used high-pressure hoses in the early morning to sluice down the dock, flushing the previous day's battle scars into the bay.

The Port Authority offices were at the entrance to the dock proper, just past the main warehousing area. After Bertram left, Charley had wandered about half way down the dock, observing the activity – mostly methodical, sometimes frantic, but never static. A commotion near the containers stacked opposite the wharfing area commanded his attention. Of particular interest was a high pitched, obviously feminine voice shouting obscenities, half in English and half in some native dialect. His pace a little more brisk, Charley altered his course to see what the commotion was about, and was surprised to find a plump elderly lady beating a young native boy with her umbrella! There were four or five others working nearby with an eye on the proceedings, but they did not interfere or stop working.

Then, as suddenly as it started, it ended. She pointed her umbrella toward the group that was still working, and the object of her attentions rushed to join in their labors. The lady glared at the group, her face a glowing red from either the exertion or from the emotion, and with her bent and bruised umbrella in hand, marched stiffly off through the stacked containers.

Charley initially thought to intervene, figuring the boy to have stolen something from her. After witnessing her effectiveness in subduing the boy, Charley was just happy to have been nothing more than a witness. Life on the docks! *Well,* he thought, *If I'm going to do anything with boats here, I'd better get used to it!*

No, it was more than just getting used to. I just saw a pecking order, one not marked with walnut desks and brass nameplates. Rather, this one was marked with raw power, brass knuckles, and fear! It dawned on him that this was one of the things he was trying to get a handle on. Who wields the power, who generates the fear, and who, if anyone, pulls their strings! As he looked over the battleground, now back to normal, he murmured almost audibly, "I've got to remember that episode, that woman!" The problem was, however, that he had been more interested in the boy being beaten than in the one inflicting the damage.

With the woman out of sight, the group, including the chastised one, was chatting lightheartedly as if nothing had happened. But they were working! There was no denying that fact.

When Charley arrived at the Majarajah, Bertram was chatting with the maitre' de. The conversation was punctuated with frequent chuckles. Charley stood behind Bert for a moment, until the maitre' de asked, "May I help you, Sir?"

Before Charley could answer, Bert turned, "Oh, Jonathan, this is the man I'm waiting for. Meet Charley Willis. You may remember him. We used to come in occasionally five or six years ago, before I got to know you and we put this deal together."

"Mr. Willis, I've heard a lot about you. Please come this way. Your table is ready. I have taken the liberty of selecting wine for you...a Rothschild..."

At the table Bert said, "Awright, dammit, what's going on? You sniffin" at something? I know you are. You don't go around the world without a reason! Now, does your reason include old Bert? Can I help you find something, get a deal on track? You know I..."

"Bert, you still talk like you were kicked out of public school in Brooklyn."

Charley recounted the Nigerian airline opportunities, and asked, "Bert, who do you remember in Lagos that may give us a handle on that business? I've got Twin

Otters and Dash 7s available, but nothing happens without a little dash. And you know better than anyone I know what happens if you dash the wrong people."

"Yes, I know. There are a few still there from our old days. There is a couple that I worked a deal with to sink a couple of old ships in the Lagos harbor loaded with concrete to use as moorings for ships waiting to unload. I'll call them tomorrow. You can talk to them. I may give too much away."

"No, you call the first time. You're just trying to confirm the story you just heard. Let that lead to their filling in details. Then we can meet with them."

Charley vowed within himself to be careful about his purpose...out to gather as much... After dinner..."Oh, by the way, there was an interesting *disturbance* on the docks after you left..." Charley went on to describe the events of the afternoon.

"Oh, you must have met our lady of the docks – Priscilla Gantz. Everyone here knows her as Pissy. She runs the docks. And you met her?"

"No, I only watched her motivate that fellow."

"Well, let me tell you, she can take care of herself. She was probably eighteen or twenty when she married this Frenchman – Pierre – I think it was Pierre Gantz. He was in the diamond business with mines upcountry out of Takado, and she traveled with him for five or six years until he determined it was too dangerous for her. It was a battle, but he won. You know, carrying diamonds over that country was getting more dangerous all the time.

So, they had this thing going with the shipping companies that Pissy took over. I guess he had to give her something to do. It was the transport of their diamonds after they had settled up with the government that started them in the transport business. Well, one thing led to another, and when Pierre was killed about eight or ten years ago –ambushed – she buried herself in the shipping business."

After a very pleasant dinner spiced with recollections of days long past, Charley became increasingly aware that Bert had not lost his ability to identify and associate with the string pullers. He said, "Bert, do you remember Percy Williams?"

"You mean Percy? From Texaco? Sure, I run into him from time to time. Why? You getting back into the wind machine business? Do you want to meet him again?"

"No, not yet, but I well may want to talk to him before I head back to the US of A!"

"If it concerns fuel in Nigeria for this aviation project you've got in mind, I think there are some possibilities to be looked at over there right now that would make what we had with Texaco look like kindergarten stuff. Why don't you bring ol' Bert up to speed? You know I can help you, particularly if you've got to be on both sides of the ocean at the same time." Bertram Amin was shrewd. It was as if he were reading Charley's mind, for the same thought was running through Charley's mind at that very moment. But Charley was not ready to bring Bert, or anyone else in yet. There was much that needed to be lined up before any general push was initiated. First, the concept of self-sufficiency needed to be sold to the Ghanaian government and Charley had the names of those administering the Senagalese contract, thanks to the *Herald Tribune*! Mr. Peter Yeboah, Managing Director of The Agricultural Development Bank of Ghana, a branch of The Bank of Ghana.

Charley thought, *That's as good a place as any right now. We need the pecking order, and I'm sure Yeboah is well versed in it. After all, no one in his right mind would allow an unranked subordinate to negotiate $15 or20 million dollar contracts.* The names mentioned in the newspaper article were not familiar to Charley, which didn't surprise him at all.

The next day, Charley called the Ag Bank and found that Peter Yeboah, as the Managing Director of the Agricultural Development Bank, had his picture prominently displayed in the Bank of Ghana's introductory brochure on the lamp table in the lobby. Peter was tall, about Charley's height and build. After the perfunctory introductions were behind them, the two men retired to a well-appointed sitting area in Yeboah's office.

The office was appointed with, apart from Yeboah's desk and its accompanying brace of chairs, a water buffalo leather sofa and two matching leather easy chairs, done in mahogany finished leather and set off toward one end of the room. Also present were two lamp tables, one on each end of the sofa and a side table beside each of the easy chairs. The other appointments included rich paintings on three of the four walls, while the fourth wall offered a view of a nicely landscaped garden through its three floor-to-ceiling windows. As Charley surveyed the settings, he slowly shook his head. *Right on.*

Three of the four committee members were available and would welcome Mr. Willis, so an impromptu meeting was set for fifteen minutes later - upstairs.

Yeboah half apologized, "We should not be long, Mr. Willis."

Charley said, "That is not a problem, I assure you. My time is yours, Mr. Yeboah. Would you prefer I wait in the outer office?"

"Not necessarily, we should be going upstairs shortly."

The setting in the upstairs offices was palatial. The three men Yeboah contacted were already together, waiting. Introductions were made all around, and a Mr. Buotto took over as chair. Yeboah brought all up to date on his conversations with Charley, and with the Bank's current interests in mind said, "Mr.Willis, earlier over the telephone, you said you envisioned a program that would make Ghana independent of Senegal, and in the process save the government millions of Cedis. Obviously, we are very interested in any program, providing it is legal, that will do what you claim. After your call, I took the basics of your proposition to those above me, and the consensus was to hear you out, which is now our pleasure. So, please continue, Mr. Willis."

"Thank you, but first, I feel a little background would be helpful, since we did not have time to put a formal business plan together. This is just the third day I've been here this trip, and the opportunity was conceived
on the trip over."

"I'm sure you have heard of our previous relations with your bank. What I have envisioned is a program where the Bank of Ghana would underwrite the acquisition of two fishing vessels and the re-positioning costs to bring them to Ghana. We have the ability to furnish experienced fishing Captains, and you could crew them with your own people drawn from the tremendous pool of talent you have right here in Tema. That would save you thirty seven million Cedis annually, according to press releases made public the past few days. Your funding would be secured by the ships to be acquired, the delivery voyage would be insured by Lloyd's of London. And a committee of this bank would pass approval on the boats and their appointments before any commitment would be binding."

"Mr. Willis, you said you had had long term relations with this bank. Could you explain that for us, please?"

"Certainly. I was the managing partner, as well as a principal, of an air freight operation known as Imperial Air Freight connecting Ghana to the United States through New York, and we used your bank as our depository for funds received here in Ghana."

"So, you are familiar with Ghana. What other business interests did you have here, at that time?"

"Well, we had very good relations with Texaco. We had a contract whereby they supplied fuel for the aircraft, and we would probably speak to them again for the fuel needed for this program, if it comes down to a 'go'."

"Mr. Willis, I can't speak for the committee, but the principal members are present in this room. If you would excuse us for a few minutes? Would you like some coffee or tea?"

"Why, yes, a cup of tea would be very bracing about now. Shall I wait in the outer area?"

Yeboah said, "Yes, we would appreciate that. I'll have your tea served there."

Charley was busy assessing the place when the tea and crumpets was served. The Ghanaians had obviously learned something from the British. Charley's eyes were drawn to several examples of Ghanaian art - at least Charley believed they were Ghanaian. One of the most imposing pieces was an elephant carved from a single piece of mahogany wood used as a coffee table base with a glass top. There were a number of lesser pieces, but that one made him stop and admire. He thought, *Something like that Vi could use in the den. I'll ask Peter where this artist lives, maybe get one on order for later. If we put this deal together.*

Charley kept reminding himself that patience is a virtue. *Just keep your cool.* It was then that Peter Yeboah stepped out to ask Charley to come back in. After being seated again, the representative from the Bank of Ghana said, "Mr. Willis, Your proposition has merit, and we want to look more closely at the program. But we need to know what these boats will cost, and what it will take money-wise to bring them over, and what the Captains salaries will be. Could you have that information for us on Monday?"

"Yes, I believe I can. I'll call the States this evening and get people working on it, but because of the time difference it will probably be Monday afternoon before they can get back to me. Whom shall I contact with the information?"

Peter Yeboah spoke, "Here's my card, please call me." There was no dissention or discussion from the group questioning Yeboah's position, a fact that was not lost on Charley.

He now had two string-pullers identified at least - Peter Yeboah and Madame "Pissy". He knew of two others he wanted on his team here in Accra. One was Bert, but he wasn't ready to let the cat out of the bag with him as yet. The other was Percy Williams. Both were very good behind-the-scenes string-pullers.

When Charley checked in with his secretary that evening, he had her open the summons to appear as a witness in Bob Murray's tax case, and to acknowledge to John Trenam that he had received the notice, and would appear. He now had most of what he needed from Ghana to get this ball rolling. He started thinking about the return flight next week and the trip to Tampa. That was going to crowd much into the week, but it was doable!

chapter three

THE CREWS ASSEMBLED

The St. Augustine restaurant was noisy, invaded by the noontime hungry. It was a poor choice for a meeting if quiet, thoughtful consideration was important, but to Charley it was perfect for the purpose of this meeting. It was the kind of place he liked, a perfect place to spring surprises. Everyone was absorbed in their own little circle, not paying much attention to those around them, and those interested in areas beyond their circle stood out and were easily identified. Yes, Charley liked this setting. And it was close to the shipyard.

But there was no clandestine purpose in this meeting, just that Charley was not only comfortable negotiating in these circumstances, he was able to use the noise and apparent confusion to his advantage. So far, everything had gone well and only one unanswered question remained: How to be sure these boats got to Africa without, of course, going aboard himself? The answer, he thought, was sitting across from him.

During a lull in the conversation, Charley offered thoughtfully, "You know, Bob, you could sail one of the boats yourself."

Bob has sensed Charley was leading up to something, but the suggestion came as a complete surprise. His jaw dropped, his eyes questioning Charley, trying to decipher the message he thought he heard. "What was that?"

Over the past two weeks, Bob and his sons had worked hard preparing the two fishing vessels, two trawlers, for delivery to Africa. During that time Charley had only been to St. Augustine twice, so the increased interest in the project both in Bob and the boys was readily apparent. He guessed they were ripe for adventure.

Bob's reaction was anticipated. Charley was right. Again.

Charley continued as if there had been no interruption.

"Sailing the Atlantic isn't much different than flying it - it just takes a little longer. Besides, you could take your sons as crew. It would be an experience they would never forget!"

Charley Willis had him hooked and Bob knew it. When Charley brought Bob's sons into the picture, all negative thoughts vanished. There was purpose beyond the present.

Charley went on about the same navigation, the same meteorology, the difference between the little twin screw Owens Bob had operated out of Clearwater and the two vessels he needed delivered to Ghana likened to small aircraft and big ones. The airplane was a transportation medium both men understood, having over thirty years flying experience each -much of that experience in the airline business.

But Bob had already made up his mind. He was going to sail the Atlantic. No. That was wrong! He and his boys were going to sail the Atlantic!

Charley was to be commended. He had done his homework, and his presentation to the government of Ghana promised to save them millions of dollars in capital outflow annually. The government jumped on it like a kid after candy, and in a matter of weeks, or in some cases, days, contracts were drawn and signed, bank accounts established, and lines of credit opened for the new venture, Alpha Fisheries, Ltd. Charley had the ball and was running hard, literally, in several directions at once. First, he needed to get the boats lined up, but he wouldn't have the time to stand over the vendor to assure their performance. Next, while in the States he wanted to arrange a market for the seafood Ghana did not want. They only wanted fish, fish for their people, but areas of the Bight of Biafra abounded with shrimp, particularly the area around the mouth of the Niger River. It was inevitable that shrimp would be part of the catch with Charley directing the operation, for a clause in his contract stated that any un-finned seafood taken – be it lobster, shrimp, or even octopus – were to be Charley's.

The possibility of marketing shrimp taken in the trawling process opened another profit center for Charley. He had already spoken with the W. R. Grace people, who immediately expressed great interest in the program Charley outlined to them particularly the transport of the seafood products after initial processing in Ghana, and held meetings with the USDA with regards to the processing requirements for such food products to enter the United States. So by the first of July, Charley's platter was pretty full. It was overflowing when you added the subpoena he had been served requiring that he testify in an IRS case involving a former employee, and later partner, Bob Murray.

chapter four

THE CREWS REUNITED

Partly as a result of Charley's testimony, Bob and Jo Murray won their four-year battle with the IRS. The IRS attempted to invoke a 100% penalty assessment in the amount of $83,000 for a company Bob had managed. Charley Willis was an investor in that company, and his testimony proved to be valuable as to the events that led to the Murray's four-year slide in the economic playground of America. Those that took that company over and attempted to fire Bob used him as a scapegoat. They had played games with withheld tax monies, then pointed their finger at others. In this case, the "others" were the Murrays. But winning with the IRS doesn't mean you get your money back! At least, that was the Murrays' experience. It was an expensive lesson – a seventeen thousand dollar lesson! Their "recovery" amounted to $48.00 and pennies! That amount represented just the court costs. The seventeen thousand was the attorney's fees. This debacle was also hanging over Bob's head when Charley made his pitch to him.

During the trial, Charley stayed with the Murrays as their houseguest. It was then that the idea light flickered on in Charley's mind. *Murray*, he thought, *Murray can handle the boats!* But because both Bob and Jo were totally absorbed in the trial, Charley thought it best not to open any discussion until the outcome was known. Besides, the nature of the outcome could affect the degree to which Bob would be interested. The more he thought about it, though, the more logical it seemed to draw Bob into the picture. So when the truth was out and the verdict in, relief flooding every corner of their being, Charley thought it an opportune time to start his plan to working. Their exhilaration was an experience unlike anything either Bob or Jo had known before. And the euphoria carried over to Charley, but not to the point where his major goals were obscured.

Bob said, "You know, there are a few days in a person's life when colors are more vivid, the air cool and still, and you feel in tune with everything around you. That's the way I feel right now. And Jo is not going to cook dinner tonight. Charley, I'm taking the three of us to Bern's Steak House in Tampa for the biggest, most tender steak we can find. Actually, I'm going to ask John if he will join us. He did a magnificent job in putting this case together."

"You go ahead and ask John, and we will go to Bern's, but the treat is on me! You've fed me, housed me, carted me around. The least I can do is participate in the celebration."

"But…"

"I insist!"

"Well..."

"Besides, Bob, I have something to discuss with you tomorrow."

John Trenam gracefully declined to join them, as his wife was recovering from surgery and he would be going to the hospital as soon as he finished at the office.

It had all started earlier that month.

The trio was still in high spirits when they arrived back home about ten. Bob's curiosity had taken hold, and he had asked Charley what he had in mind to talk about. Charley outlined the Ghana program in general terms. He told them that one of his missions to Florida was to locate ships for Alpha Fisheries, Ltd.

"Have you lined up your ships yet, Charley?"

"Yes, in a way. I've talked to the people who have the Black Angus boats in Lantana. They're for sale, and I would like to see them. I thought we might take your airplane over there and check them out."

"Charley, if you're talking about the boats I think you're talking about, there is a man here in Clearwater who used to fly for me at National Aviation. He was Captain of the Black Angus, fishing for lobster in south Caribbean waters."

"Can we talk to him?"

"Certainly, if he's in town. I'll call him in the morning. It's a little late to rattle his cage tonight."

That evening, their second son Rick and his wife Bobi stopped by the house for a dip in the pool, and a chance to see Charley. Rick knew little of the project Charley was pursuing, but he was appreciative of Charley's part in resolving the IRS situation. Charley had watched all the boys grow into young men and this was Rick's opportunity to say hello. He didn't know how long Charley would be in town and he didn't want to miss him.

As they strolled up the brick walk to the front door, Rick said, "You'll like Charley. He's been like a second father to us, particularly when Dad was in the airline. Steve and I went to Alaska once when he was on board, and the stewardesses had us serving cokes and coffee. Charley thought that was hilarious."

The front door was a massive carved wood production, part of a major remodeling job his dad undertook to capitalize on the house's spectacular location. The entrance walkway wound through a small garden area featuring three tall coconut palms, hidden lights illuminating them in hues of red, green, and yellow. On the left of the entrance garden was the new master bedroom addition, with its own shallow inset garden nestled behind three Spanish style archways, also faintly illuminated by hidden lights. Setting at a slight angle to the right of the entrance garden was the pre-renovation attached garage. Once you set foot on the walk, the real world was lost. It was as though you were entering a feature pavilion at Disney World. Even the sounds of civilization were muted.

The setting encouraged you to leave your cares behind, something Bob never accomplished while the IRS charges hung over his head. The boys hoped that would pass now that the issue was settled. Every time Rick came "home" at night he marveled at the transformation of the property, and the transformation that it seemed to work in him. Tonight was no exception.

The Spanish motif continued inside the house, with arches and iron accents on mirrored walls, but these decorating touches were overshadowed by the view. Stepping out of the foyer into the family area between the living room on the left and the dining area on the right, the eye was captured by the view across the poolside patio down the waterway. The house stood on a point of land separating two waterways. From the patio, you looked westward down the major waterway to the inter-coastal one-eighth of a mile distant. The smaller of the waterways ran off a short distance to the right. All the properties were sea-walled, many with docking facilities and boats tied to them. The 30-foot Owens was tied to the Murrays' dock.

And the pelicans guarded the territory.

One the other side of the inter-coastal waterway ran a line of long thin islands standing as defenders from the storms that occasionally plague the Gulf of Mexico, their palm trees standing as a row of proud infantry, their mangroves the barracks for the herons, cranes, ibis, and pelicans.

Rick knocked politely, then opened the door for Bobi.

"Hi. It's only us, " Rick announced.

"Come on in, we've been expecting you," Jo said. "Charley and your Dad are on the patio going over some things."

"We were by an hour ago, but you weren't home, so we went shopping. Thought we'd try once more on our way home. I hadn't seen Mr. Willis yet."

Bobi went into the kitchen to offer her help, while Rick headed for the two men engrossed in papers spread over the patio table. Sandi was in the pool, swimming. To watch her, no one would believe she grew up deathly afraid of water. At three years of age, she was tumbled end over teacup by a breaker on the beach at Long Beach, Washington, an experience that invoked uncontrollable screams as a child any time she was threatened by the thought of entering the water. But for all of the eleven years they were in Florida, all three of the homes they had were with swimming pools. Primarily because of her brothers' help, she graduated first to waterwings, then from waterwings. Now, at fifteen, she held all the grace of a ballerina in the water.

As Rick slid the patio door open, both men looked up. Bob said, "Hi Rick. Pull up a chair. You may be interested in this."

"What is it?"

"Charley has a deal in Africa to set up a fishing operation there. He's asked me to help locate two trawlers for him. The University breaks for the summer in what? Two weeks?"

"Yeah, May 24th…why?"

"We were thinking that you boys might like to make a little extra cash when school is out."

"No argument there!"

Walt came in soon afterward and joined the patio conference. Within the hour, Charley had his team. Dan would be back from Tallahassee in about two weeks, and to the best of everyone's knowledge, had no commitments made for the summer. Walt and Rick both went to the University of South Florida, although at different campuses, and jumped at the chance to work with their dad.

Charley had all he wanted and signaled the end of the business conference with, "I need a drink." He poured a stiff scotch and swirled the amber liquid slowly in his glass and smiled to himself. The warm glow he felt inside was only partly scotch. No, it was more the fact that fate had apparently dealt him a winning hand again. He would make money on this deal. Lots of it.

The next morning dawned cloudless, with little wisps of fog hanging like orphans with no visible means of support over the mirror surface of the waterway. Bob was on the patio with a cup of coffee, his mind now trying to organize some sort of game plan to put their lives back in order. He found four years of frustration was difficult to bury, but the peacefulness of the scene dulled the pain that had so often tried his patience. A lone pelican stood motionless on the dock piling, like a self-appointed guardian of tranquility. Bob thought, "If that's what you are up to, you're doing a good job of it."

"Good morning."

Bob was so lost in thought that Charley's greeting startled him.

"Good morning, Charley. I'm sorry, I didn't hear you get up. Guess I was trying to get the day organized. Let me get you a cup of coffee, and I'll call Carl."

"No, Bob, I'm going to hold off on the coffee for a while, but go ahead and call your man. Let's see when we can get together with him."

Bob called Carl Jenson, who agreed to meet with them later that morning. While waiting for Jenson, talk drifted to alternatives to buying the aluminum hulled Black Angus boats. Bender shipyards in Mobile built steel hulled vessels, and St. Augustine Trawlers had a good reputation for wooden hulled ships, several of which still hunted shrimp out of Tarpon Springs. The more they talked, the more obvious it became that a review of these alternatives should be included in Charley's plans.

Walt joined them, sitting quietly trying to develop an understanding of what was involved. The more he listened, the more excited he became inwardly. Walt had always loved boats and would often take the 20' catamaran out to the coastal islands – sometimes with one or two neighbor boys, sometimes on his own. The sea seemed to hold a magnetic attraction to him.

Walt was twenty, in his second year at University of South Florida. Business Administration was his chosen field, with a data processing minor. His was an inventive mind, with a natural flair for the mechanical or technical challenges confronting him. As a child, he made many of his own toys, including a rubber band-powered cannon with a barrel of spools from his mother's sewing basket when he was ten. Initially, the projectiles were pencil stubs - short, used wooden pencil stubs that his "cannon" could fire all the way across the room. He would occupy himself for hours setting up targets for bombardment, within a set of guidelines set down by his mother. The guidelines only defined where he could shoot, and what he could shoot at. Those guidelines failed to limit the range of weaponry his mind could conceive.

His adolescent military exercises came to an abrupt halt when Jo found him shooting live shells into the fireplace from across the room! The "live shells" had been made of three or four "strike anywhere matches" bound together with thread. When these matches landed, they would, of course, ignite. It was this smell of warfare that brought Jo out of the kitchen, with a resulting cessation of Walt's war. SALT 3 was implemented in an instant and the weapons destroyed, reduced to spools, pencil stubs and matches again.

Later, Bob and the other boys were to appreciate his inventiveness.

When the doorbell rang the conversation had lightened with Charley and Bob recalling some of their experiences in Alaska and in Africa. Walt said, "I'll get it."

"If it's Carl, bring him out here and get him coffee, please."

A deeply tanned athletic type was ushered to the patio, a shock of dark hair graying at the temples and blue eyes framed in laughing crow's feet made him instantly likeable.

"Carl," Bob said, "you remember Charley. He was one of the owners of the flight school. He was here several times while you were flying with us there."

"Yes. It's Mr. Willis, isn't it?"

"You have a good memory, Carl."

"Well, I don't think I was ever formally introduced, but everyone knew who you were when you came in."

"Carl, Bob tells me you ran one of the Black Angus boats. I've had a couple of them offered to me for a client of mine. You were part of the crew?"

"You could say that. I was the captain of the Black Angus."

"That should qualify you, perhaps for a lot of things. What can you tell me about those boats?"

"You know they are aluminum hulls, don't you?"

"Yes. Why?"

"Well, aluminum itself is not so bad, but the Angus people took a pleasure boat hull, a shallow vee hull, and made a work boat out of it. It's fast in calm or moderate water, but in heavy seas it will ride to the top of the wave, then fall off hard in the trough. We had problems with seams splitting if the boat hits the bottom of the trough very hard. The problem was in trying to find a place to repair the damage, since aluminum requires special welding equipment."

"If you were buying a boat to fish with, would the Lantana boat or boats be your first choice? Forget the welding problem."

Carl said, "No, I think I'd look for one designed as a fisher or trawler from the beginning."

Charley thought for a moment, then said, "I don't think the Angus boats are going to go anywhere for a few days, Bob. Let's call that outfit in St. Augustine and the one in Mobile. Are you free to fly over there if they have anything to talk about?"

"Not at the moment, Charley, but I believe I can shuffle things around. When did you want to go?"

"Just as soon as we can find something to talk about with someone who has a couple of boats for sale. We'll cover your costs and your time, Bob."

chapter five

BOB MURRAY VS. THE IRS

Meanwwhile, back in the Tampa/Largo environs, Bob Murray was drawing ever closer to a confrontation in court over some $83,000 the IRS claimed he was responsible for not paying to the government, representing withholding taxes of some 85 employees of a successful flight school founded by Murray, with Charley and Howard Bell as partners. Upon the recommendation of his attorney for the Flight School, William Bussey, he had agreed with Mr. John Trenam, Esq., of Tampa to defend him. John Trenam was a master when it came to tax law, and he needed every bit of insight gained in forty years working for and against the IRS to come up with the key to the action that had been brought against Bob. In setting up the case, Bob paid the taxes for one of his employees, then sued the government for recovery of the amounts paid - which monies he never recovered.

For three years John had chased false reports, and had attended terminal meetings with the IRS that "should close this issue," only to be followed in another six months with a request to bring all documents and records to an IRS office of higher authority. On a hunch, John had sent a junior attorney to the Federal Archives in Atlanta. He returned with a copy of an agreement between the IRS and Howard Bell relieving Bell of any further withholding taxes not yet paid over by Bell's company. Bob had been President of that company, but had left prior to the time tax funds were redirected to another of Wells' interests. The uncovered agreement and Charley's testimony absolved Bob of any wrongdoing.

John Trenam warned Bob, "These documents and affidavits support your claim, but remember, you are not suing Howard Bell, you are suing the United States of America. Did you get hold of Charley Willis? We only have five weeks before the trial. That's not a lot of time for all we have yet to do."

"Yes, I know. Charley is still in Africa, but I talked to his office and told his secretary what is happening, and I told her about the summons so there would be no surprises. Charley's wife said he is there on a business trip and is due back in two or three weeks. She said there would not be a problem for a May trip to Florida, because he has promised to take the family to Disney World, and this would be a perfect way of keeping him to his promise. I know Charley, and there is bad blood between him and Howard. Howard cost him over a half million dollars, a good bit of that going into Howard's pocket."

"You think, then, that Charley will be here?"

"Yes, and he will call us as soon as he gets back in the States, if not before. His wife will see to that."

When Charley did get back, he did call Bob, as he said he would and outlined his schedule which included arriving in Tampa a week before the planned visit to Disney World. Bob agreed to meet him at the airport, and extended a new invitation to stay with the Murrays during the trial. Bob was well acquainted with Charley's drinking habits, having earned the name of "Whiskey" Willis as a Naval airman during WW II. Old habits are hard to break, especially if there is not a heart to make the change. So Bob opted to reduce the influence the firewater had in Charley's life until after the trial was past. But Charley brought his own bottle. That control could best be done if Charley was close at hand with many adolescent wardens hovering around him, and there were a stable full of them at Bob's home in the form of his sons.

Charley was very agreeable, recounting to Bob on the way home, some of the problems he encountered in Tema, including the experience of Pissy Gantz on the dock. Charley thought that is one that Bob ought to know about, since if Charley had his way Bob would run into her down the line somewhere.

So Bob quit laughing long enough to ask, "Are all the women so macho over there?"

"No, but those that are make you appreciate those that aren't even more!

chapter six

ST. AUGUSTINE TRAWLERS

That evening on the patio, Charley partially unfolded his plan. Ever cautious, he always held enough back to make sure he was on solid ground when shifts in strategy were indicated He had a commitment from the Bank of Ghana including a promise to wire transfer $250,000 U.S. dollars into Riggs National Bank in Washington, DC, where Charley was very well known, for the purpose of acquiring two fishing trawlers for deployment to Ghana. There was much more legal language in the agreement, including a provision that a representative of the bank of Ghana be designated to administer the funding. Mr. Yeboah was appointed by the committee to be liaison for them in this venture. He was currently in Washington working out the final details of the transfer and the draw down procedures to be employed to draw on the account.

"Just plan on being busy for the next week or so. Carl, I still want to see the Lantana boats. If you don't mind, I may call you again before we go over there."

"That won't be a problem, Mr. Willis. If it would help, I could possibly go over with you."

"Thanks, Carl, that may help. We've got some calls to make before we can put a schedule together, but I'll let you know what's happening."

St. Augustine Trawlers painted a very promising picture with a list of references operating their vessels including those operating out of Tarpon Springs, just ten miles north of Bob's home. After Charley hung up with St. Augustine, he tried to call some of the references, being successful in only one instance. But the glowing report offered was enough motivation to cancel all other plans and fly to St. Augustine.

"Bob, you said you could shuffle your schedule; could you shuffle it for tomorrow?"

"I'm sure I can, Charley. The only meeting I have for tomorrow would probably be more convenient for everyone if we met on Saturday. I'll call as soon as we know what you want to do."

"Well, that's easy. I want to go to St. Augustine!"

It took over an hour, but Bob was able to clear his appointments for the remainder of the week.

He didn't want to appear too eager, so Charley didn't call back to St. Augustine until late afternoon. Jerry Thompson apparently wasn't concerned about impressions and offered to meet them at the airport at nine o'clock the next morning.

Charley said, "We can call you when we get on the ground in the morning."

"Did I understand you are coming by private plane? Landi0ng i0n St. Augustine?"

"That's right."

"Well, if you fly down the river, you will see us on the east bank. Just circle the yard and I'll head for the airport. You expect to be here about nine?"

"We may be a little earlier, say eight-thirty?"

"That's all right, Mr. Willis. Call me if you have a problem. Otherwise I'll be looking for you at eight-thir....well, anytime after eight is OK by me. I'll see you when you come by."

"OK."

That night in bed, Jo asked, "What is Charley up to? He's got something going in Africa?"

"Yes, it looks that way. He's cut some sort of deal with the Ghana government to set up a fishing operation over there. I'll find out more tomorrow. He's trying to locate two fishing boats and wants me to fly him around to look at them. But, listen, this is no time to talk about business!"

"Yes," she smiled, "I agree." Bob was smiling, too, as he turned out the light.

The next morning, a check with Flight Service showed the entire east coast of Florida was affected by a common weather system. Jacksonville was reporting 4000' overcast, as was Daytona. Vero Beach had 1800' broken and a 4000' ceiling. Miami had a measured 1600' ceiling. The local area at St. Petersburg reported a 6000' broken layer and another one at 12,000'. Bob filed a visual flight plan, figuring to stay under the weather, circumnavigating the showers.

The flight from Clearwater to St. Augustine was uneventful. The showers were widely spaced, adding a freshness to the morning landscape that sparkled, even under overcast skies. The early morning traffic on Interstate 75 traveling with lights on contributed to the illusion. Nearing the east coast, the skies darkened and the illusion faded, but the ceiling stayed a comfortable 4000', 2500' above them as they flew down the St. John's River. Charley wanted to locate the shipyard from the air before landing, which proved to be no problem at all.

"There it is, Bob!" Charley exclaimed. The main building was marked "ST. AUGUSTINE TRAWLERS" in yellow block letters on both faces of the roof. That, and the fact that the buildings were separated from other industry in the area made it stand out clearly. The eye was naturally drawn to it like gravy on a silk tie.

As they circled, Charley could see one hull on the ways outside the building and another coming up from the keel inside the building. There were no boats at the dock.

"Look over there, on the other side of the river." Bob pointed to another shipyard with much more activity. "There must be five, no, six boats in the water, and they look like the one on the ways at the Trawlers." Charley had that familiar inner feeling that this trip was the right choice.

"Jerry's going to meet us at the airport, but maybe we can visit this other one after the meeting with Jerry...I knew you had some options, Charley, but I didn't expect to find them next door to each other."

Jerry drove up as they entered the small building that served as office, terminal, and general store. "Mr. Willis?"

"Yes," Charley responded, "And you would be Jerry Thompson? Please call me Charley. And this is Bob Murray." They all shook hands and Jerry spoke "Thank you. Glad to meet you both. I gathered from your conversation yesterday that you have a deadline on getting some boats on order, so may I suggest we go straight to the yard."

Charley said, "Jerry, you're my kind of man!"

"My car is over here. The yard is only fifteen minutes away."

Identifying the other shipyard was as easy as spotting the Trawlers, since the two were operating in each other's front yard. The other boats were clearly visible from the St. Augustine works, languishing at their dock only a hundred yards away. Jerry made the job easier.

"That's the Desco yard over there. I used to work for them," Jerry said, pointing across the river. "Our boats look like twins from a distance, and in many ways are the same. The same length, same beam, same tackle. But it's the hidden differences that set us apart."

He explained that he and his partners had redesigned the hull, adding three-fourths of a knot to cruise speed. When you are talking three hundred to four hundred knots, three-fourths of a knot isn't measurable. But speeding up from nine to almost ten knots, almost a ten percent increase, that's something you can measure at the fuel pit after a week's fishing.

"We start with a solid oak keel and a unique prow. We cut the water better, and will take less green water over the bow in heavy seas. Come inside here, I'll show you what I mean."

Inside the boathouse, the bare skeleton Charley had spotted from the air did look like it may one day become a ship; it held that promise, but not much more. The fact that it was lying there like a disemboweled dinosaur made the visualization of Jerry's claims easy to understand, however. It was as though the beast had rolled over on its back and wasted away until all that was left was a backbone and some ribs stretching skyward. The graceful curves flowing back from the prow were just beginning to take shape as the first layer of planking was added. Both men appreciated streamlining, a necessity in efficient aircraft design. The effect of the sweeping lines reaching back from the bow was not lost on them.

"The biggest change is here in the bow. See how the lines flow to a point at the bow?" Jerry didn't wait for an answer, adding, "The Desco hull 'pooches out' at the bow like a balloon with a stick in front. That makes the boat push a lot more water, and that takes fuel and cuts your speed. The fact that we push much less water means there is less piled up in front waiting to come aboard when you bury the bow. That, and the little flare we introduced in the bow lines makes a remarkable difference in the amount of water you take, because as the bow starts under, the flare offers lift to keep it up."

"Now I'd like to show you how this all comes together." Jerry led them through the maze of timbers, hoses, and lines to the boat on the ways outside the building. As they approached the vessel, its size became increasingly impressive.

The ship was cradled on blocks resting in turn on a long steel cart. The pair of rails supporting the cart disappeared into the St. John River. The wheels of the cart were chocked to prevent premature launching. Additional shoring sprouted like rows of tall corn along each side of the boat.

"All of this is removed when we're ready to launch," Jerry said, waving his hand to take in all the supporting structures. "The trolley is held back by that cable tied to the cart and by the chocks under the wheels. The winch at the head of the boathouse is primarily used to recover the trolley, so we release the cable and then knock the chocks out holding the trolley. After the boat floats off, we recover the trolley with the winch and cable."

The laying on of the planking was clearly seen from under the hull. As each plank is laid up and secured, the gap is caulked with oakum, a fibrous material soaked in tar and resin.

Jerry explained, "The gap between the planks is necessary because, once the boat is in the water, the wood will swell. We have to leave room for it to swell, or the hull planking will buckle with a leak to fix, involving dry-dock and re-planking. I guess you could say you have to leave it loose to make it tight."

The deck was about sixteen feet above the ground, but looking up the ladder, it looked at least twice that far. On deck, the basic simplicity of the ship was everywhere. There were no masts, no stays or guys, no winch...just a wide expanse of uncluttered deck behind the deckhouse. But the opportunity to study the basic structure created an invaluable confidence as to the integrity of the vessel in both men's minds.

She was seventy-three feet long. The foredeck was only about eleven feet in length, bounded aft by the rounded face of the wheelhouse. A hatch leading downward into the forepeak below was located in the center of this deck, the hatch being hinged on the forward side to prevent seas coming over the bow from loosening the hatch cover and washing it away.

The face of the wheelhouse itself looked like an oversized bow window, the kind you see in dining and living rooms of some larger houses. It wasn't really rounded, but was a series of flat sections, each one sporting a window and each one angled a little more to the rear until the side of the house paralleled the run of the ship. A hatch the size of a narrow door was set in each side of the wheelhouse sliding aft to open. A latch on the forward side secured the hatch in the closed position, and a simple hook and eyelet kept it in place when open.

Inside, the wheelhouse was elevated above the deck, both to improve visibility since the bow of the ship rose noticeably and the prow would be in the line of vision from the normal deck level, and also to provide a positive means of clearing water from the wheelhouse in heavy seas. Bob was to learn later how important this feature really was. "Green water" coming over the bow can carry enough power to break or displace the forward windows in the wheelhouse allowing a torrent of water to rush in. The elevated deck allows that water to run off without help. When you're taking water over the bow, you don't have much time for housekeeping.

In the center against the forward bulkhead was the helm. The compass occupied the most prominent place, in front of everything. The oak wheel, mounted on the aft face of the helm, was about thirty-six inches in diameter. Its eight spokes were crowned by eight oaken handles extending beyond the rim. These handles not only made it easy to control the helm, but with two straps, called Beckett straps, one attached to each side of the helm and looped over the handle on top, the wheel can be immobilized. This is an indispensable device when running in reverse, since water flowing backwards over the rudder can create unusually high and totally unexpected forces on the wheel.

On the console's upper face are engine gauges, throttle control and reverse shift lever, and an autopilot engage lever. The designers were careful to leave enough room for coffee cups and ashtrays, devices thought to help combat tedium.

"The wheelhouse looks pretty empty right now," Jerry said. "And it won't be much different when everything is installed. Your VHF ship to ship radio will be over the wheel, and electrical control panels will be mounted on the aft bulkhead where those cables are. You'll have a captain's chair bolted down on the starboard side, and that's it! The rest of your radios will be below in the captain's cabin."

The sliding hatch in the center of the aft bulkhead led into the captain's cabin. The cabin was actually two steps below the wheelhouse level, allowing for a row of fixed glass panes across the back of the wheelhouse. The view aft was not spectacular, but was sufficient for general maneuvering in harbor waters. The helmsman could pick up hand signals from deck crew without leaving the wheel. The only view aft in a flat wheelhouse design is gained by stepping outside!

Everything in the captain's cabin was built in. On the port side was the bunk, about three feet above the deck with lockers below. Just inside the cabin on the starboard side was a chart table with chart lockers below and a rack above which Jerry explained was for ship to shore radios. "Weep holes" in the floor allowed water entering the cabin to drain below to the bilges.

The rear of the cabin was covered with built-in clothes lockers and drawers, and a desk adorned the starboard bulkhead. A windowed ventilation hatch similar to those in the wheelhouse was centered on the outside wall above the bunk. This hatch, like the forward ones, was either on or off, open or closed. There was no in between!

The sheer bulk of the ship was not as impressive from the deck as it had been from below, and was made even less so by the cramped arrangement of the captain's cabin. But the thought of the hold and up to twenty thousand pounds of fish... that was impressive.

The rest of the morning was spent reviewing options, design features, delivery schedules, and price. Jerry surprised everyone by revealing St. Augustine Trawlers had boats working as far away as India.

"Jerry, this has been an eye-opening experience." Charley continued, "When I called you yesterday, I had no idea what we would find here. I am impressed. What do you say to continuing this over lunch?"

"Sounds good to me. If you like seafood, there's a very good place not far away."

[They all agreed, and Charley thought this might be an ideal time to tie Bob down. After all, he did need to get someone on board to deliver the boats, someone he could trust. The St. Augustine restaurant was noisy, invaded by the noontime hungry. It was another excellent spot for a meeting if quiet, thoughtful consideration was not important, except to Charley. It was perfect for the underlying purpose of this meeting. It was tailormade for Charley, the kind of place he liked. Everyone was relaxed all but Charley. To him, this was another information gathering session. He allowed time to soften the Jerry's thinking, relax him as well Then Charley offered him a carrot,"Jerry, we have a budget we must work within, could you put some numbers together for us on a basic 73 foot boat like the one we just saw, with enough fuel to get from here to Africa?"

Jerry replied, "Well,I can tell you the one you saw went for a little over $ 127,000. Qf course, you will have some extras, and we will have to figure the fuel capacity and size the tanks required."

"That's all right, I just wanted to be sure we're in the ball park. Charley primarily wanted to get some ballpark figures for use with Desco or Bender whenever he got the chance to sit down with them.
With Bob on board, the next step would be much simpler At present, Jerry seemed to be a lost cause, because of the completion schedules.

There was no clandestine purpose in this meeting, just that Charley was not only comfortable negotiating in these circumstances, he was able to use the noise and apparent confusion to his advantage. So far, everything had gone well, but only one unanswered question remained: How to be sure these boats got to Africa? Without, of course, going aboard himself. The answer, he thought, was sitting across from him.

During a lull in the conversation, Charley offered thoughtfully, "You know, Bob, you could sail one of the boats yourself and your boys could go as crew! Just an off-hand comment, but it had its effect." Bob said, "Yes, it would be an education to them,[ ] provided the boys are willing and we can convince their mother that it's best for them. I'm sure the boys will be gung ho, but I think we'll have to do a sales job on their mother.

At lunch, Jerry agreed to price out the options Charley had selected. Charley wanted to set up the radio and electronic equipment himself since both he and Bob had contacts with a number of suppliers and could get as good a price as Jerry, without his overhead.

And while the accommodations were not Waldorf Astoria, air conditioning was considered desirable. It would keep the radios somewhat drier and freer of corrosion.

There seemed to be a cloud on the conversation when it got down to price and terms. Charley's "deal" with the Ghanaians revolved around favorable terms, especially during construction. The original plan was to acquire a used vessel, in which case a viable entity would exist from the day the papers were signed to show for the monies laid out. For a ship that existed only on paper, the Ghanaians were a little reluctant to lay any substantial amount of cash on the line to a company half a world away, regardless of who endorsed the deal. Their money was on deposit with Riggs Bank in Washington, D.C., and Charley had direct access to it, but limitations were imposed as to how it should be spent.

Jerry admitted the two boats St. Augustine had on the ways were already committed, pegging sail-away for Charley about four months down the pike if this deal was cut then and there.

"Jerry, that's going to be our biggest problem. I have only three months left to get some ships into Africa, and working! My people were expecting a used vessel, and even with refurbishing, it could be in service within two months. The Ghanaians don't care what it looks like, as long as it is priced right and it brings in fish. Before I tell them that we can't deliver as we agreed, I've got to look at the used boat options."

"I understand that, Charley, but I think you're going to be far happier with new rather than used."

The conversation turned to polite, pre-departure chatter, during which Jerry offered to drive them back to the airport. On the way, Jerry said, "You know, we would really like to sell you two boats, but there's no way we can come close to the delivery schedule you need. If you haven't already thought of it, why don't you call Desco? You're sure to find something somewhere that comes close. And since you're going back on the trail, you might as well start looking here. They're good people, and if they can't help you, they may be able to point you to someone who could."

"Thanks, Jerry. That's a good idea. Hmm. You know, Bob, it's only 1:45. We would have time today to find out what they could do in the used market. Just drop us at the airport, if it's not too much trouble."

"It's no trouble at all. The airport is almost on the way back."

"I'll stay in touch, particularly in the event Desco can't locate any used vessels for us. There may be something that will pop up on your radar screen in the meantime."

"Dick Bennett is their president. I've got his number in my day timer. I'll get it for you when we get to the airport unless you want to stop and call him now."

"Thanks anyway, Jerry. If he were there, it wouldn't seem proper to have you drop us at your competitor's. If he's interested in who we've talked to, he'll ask. Thanks again."

At the airport, Charley called Desco.

chapter seven

DESCO SHIPBUILDING CORPORATION

Desco was one of the shipbuilding enterprises of the California based Whittaker Corporation. The other was Bertram Yachts of Miami. When Charley called, the response was straightforward and business-like, yet the soft, smiling voice at the other end started drawing pleasant pictures in the mind.

"Good afternoon, is Mr. Bennett in?"

"Who is calling, please?"

"Charles Willis."

"I'm sorry, Mr. Willis, but I am told Mr. Bennett left the yard for a short time. Could you please call back, or is there a number where he could reach you?"

"I would be happy to call back, Ma'am, but I just want to buy some boats. Perhaps there is someone else I could talk to?"

The voice changed. It was the emotional difference between a strikeout and a home run! It turned out that all their marketing people were out on calls, so the Voice offered to send a car for the two men. Desco apparently had a drill they exercised in those situations: "Get the net. Don't let a live one get away!"

As soon as she hung up from Charley's call, Angie called one of the accounting staff. "Allan, there are two men at the airport, a Mr. Willis and a Mr. Murray, to see Mr. Bennett. Please pick them up. It's important." The Voice was still soft, but a hint of authority replaced a little of the smile.

"Which airport, Angie? Jacksonville?"

"No, they're right here in St. Augustine."

"OK, I'm gone."

When Allan returned to the shipyard with the two men, Dick Bennett was waiting. He opened the car door. "Mr. Willis?"

"Charley Willis. Just call me Charley."

As Bob walked around the other side of the car, Bennett said, "And you would be Mr. Murray."

"Yes, better known as 'Bob'."

"Good to meet you. I'm Dick Bennett. My secretary tells me you're interested in some boats?"

Dick appeared to be in his forties, a sandy haired ebullient fellow with a ruddy complexion, stocky build, and sharp blue eyes. His height was not intimidating - at five-eight or nine, he appeared almost dwarfed by Charley's six plus feet. Bob stood five foot ten and matched Dick's build. Dick didn't just have a smile. He radiated friendliness with his whole face. His eyes sparkled. They weren't the eyes of a cold, calculating businessman, a trait that had thrown a number of deal-seekers off guard. They invited your friendliness in return.

Charley Willis was no slouch in negotiations. He was unusually adept at reading people, perhaps a result of dual degrees in both Business Administration and Psychology. He had been an advisor on the White House staff under Eisenhower, and had served fourteen years as president of an international flag airline. These were also traits the Bank of Ghana found attractive when they considered the proposal Charley had placed before them.

Usually, Charley structured an in-depth file on the person with whom he would be dealing - what his interests were, even to the sports teams he followed. High school, college, and post-graduate institutions were all information targets that, once mentioned in conversation, were locked away in Charley's mind for future use. Even the type of perfume worn by the wives of these people did not escape his interest. Long before, when they were dealing on an overseas contract, Bob had asked him about this penchant for background on everyone. Charley's simple answer was, "The only information you can't use is that which you don't have."

With Dick Bennett, he was starting with a blank sheet. But he started filling it in when the receptionist first answered the telephone. "It's amazing," he would say, "how much the employee reflects the boss."

Their gaze swept the shipyard. From the drive in front of the single story administration building, they could not see the dock area. To their right, however, was a two-story warehouse-type building, and immediately behind it extending toward the river was a larger, taller building which contained four sets of ways. Left of the administration building was a fenced yard storage area and a series of specialty shops including cabinetry or woodworking, electrical, plumbing, and welding. These shops' production fed into the area behind the administration building for incorporation into the vessel (or vessels) under construction on the ways, or in finishing operations at the dock. Specialty shop production output was closely monitored and controlled; otherwise, a traffic jam of major proportions would occur at Bennett's feet.

Bob murmured to Charley, "Looks like they went big league. Wonder what they could put out in full production?"

Dick said, "We'll get a look at the plant later, but first, let's go into my office. It would help to know exactly what you are looking for." As they walked inside, Dick continued, "We have a good variety of fishing boats in both wood and fiberglass hulls," pointing out pictures of various designs along the hallway walls.

By the time they sat down in Dick's office Charley Willis had formed a mental profile of the man seated across from him. The conversation to that point had been extremely one-sided, with Bennett putting his sales personality in high gear, a fact that was not lost on Charley. He thought, *There's more to this than just wanting to sell a couple of boats. They NEED to sell them!*

"Mr. Bennett...err...I'm sorry, Dick, we are looking for two vessels to operate in foreign waters, trawling primarily for fish. I'll admit, we first saw your operation from the air today, so we come totally unprepared as to the capacity of your vessels to meet our needs, your production capacity, or your financial standing. I don't even have a Dun & Bradstreet on you. So, if you would, could you please give us little background on Desco?"

"Certainly. We are owned by the Whittaker Corporation and as such, enjoy very sound financial footing. You do know the Whittaker Corporation, don't you?"

"No, not really." Charley did know of the company, but this was not the time to head Bennett off.

"That's not a problem, I assure you. I'll get you a copy of our last financial statements before you leave today." Dick rang for Angie and asked that a complete financial package be put together for Charley, then continued, "Now, I need to know what you want, in as much detail as you can give me. Generally speaking, there isn't much in the field from forty to eighty-three feet that we can't provide. Each of our basic designs offers a variety of options relating to type of catch, geographical area, and the length of the tour."

Bennett didn't give Charley a chance to reply as he went on, "Production wise, if you could use something in the seventy-three foot range, I have one in the water and another on the ways that are not sold yet. These are wood hulls that can be fitted with your choice of options except engines. Both will have Caterpillar D343 engines, which are on hand. Both boats have fuel enough for about a month's fishing, about nine or ten thousand gallons each. Would these interest you?"

Charley was, again, smiling inside as he said, "They may. If these ships will do the job for us, it will depend on the price and terms as to whether there is an interest."

Bob had remained quiet. Now he began to see what Charley was doing, recruiting Dick Bennett as Alpha Fisheries salesman to sell a financing package to Desco's banks, or to the parent company. Charley Willis didn't care which. "What do you mean by terms, Charley? We normally require half the purchase price at signing, and the balance at delivery."

Charley replied, "I could understand that if you were starting one from the keel up. But you have two vessels nearing completion with a substantial investment already committed and I have limitations imposed by the government we represent as to the funds at my disposal. I would like to think some common ground could be found, providing the price was acceptable and the vessels are suitable."

"These funds, they are in the United States?"

"Yes. They are on deposit with Riggs Bank in Washington, D.C."

"Then I think we can work something out. If you like, we could take a short tour around the yard, and look the boats over, you know, to get a better idea as to how these boats would fit your program."

As they left the office, Dick pointed out their purchasing and stores building, the large warehouse-type structure off to the left of the administration building. "We will set a secure area aside in that building for your on board stores. They will be on hand but out of the way until you are ready to board them." Bob thought, *What a way to start a tour...eliminate your problems before they become problems.*

Logistics can create headaches of migraine proportions even if you do know what you are doing. Those first steps into the yard made both men realize there was much to learn about outfitting a new vessel for an ocean crossing. They would need help and here, that help was considered part of the sale package! Of course, Bennett did not yet know the vessels were destined for Africa.

Bob said, "How much room is available in that building?"

"We have several lockup areas, any one of which could hold all you could conceive to put on board."

"Will they hold a car?" Bob asked.

"A car?!" Dick was at first incredulous, then fascinated.

"Well," Charley offered, "It's actually a Buick station wagon – the small one."

"Where are you taking these boats that you'd take your own wheels along?"

"Would you believe West Africa?" Charley replied.

"Yes, that wouldn't surprise me at all. We have boats working all over the world, and, incidentally, provide parts support for them. We have short wave radio contact with most of our overseas customers. West Africa would be no problem on the twenty-three meter band."

Bob said, "Dick, it sounds like you've been down this road many times before. Do you have a list – a master list – of the supplies and spares we might need for an ocean crossing?"

"Sure. We can get a general list from our purchasing people. But first, I'd like to show you a finished boat. It's due to be picked up this week to go to Paramaribo, Suriname. It's been out on sea trials, and we're just tweaking up a few items."

There were five vessels tied to the dock. Two had another tied alongside. Dick pointed out the single tied at the end of the line.

As if on cue, the sun broke through the overcast.

She sparkled. She was solid white, dazzling white in the sun, with black outriggers, rigging, and stack. Black window frames and a black edging around the deckhouse overhang set the deckhouse off. The deck itself was a gray vinyl-like material with a non-skid finish. The double drummed winch squatted immediately behind the deckhouse and was, like the outriggers, painted a shiny black. Fresh grease peeked out from the bearings. The steel cable had been wound, and was still factory bright on the spool.

Three white life rings were secured to the side of the deckhouse, and a bright orange life raft rested on top of the deckhouse. It was as though the artist that conjured this picture decided to add one accent - one splash of color to complete his masterpiece.

But this was not a thoroughbred. It was a workhorse. In the scene before them, however, it took on the character of the Clydesdales in the Budweiser ads. Today, it was an art form!

By the time they reached that ship, both men had developed a feeling that the Desco people would be very easy to work with. They seemed to appreciate myriad details so easily overlooked, and appeared genuinely interested in more than the sale and delivery of a vessel. Their seeming interest lay in getting their vessels to work, to be put on display in the workboat arena - an advertisement they didn't have to pay for.

Their concern for a safe voyage was not shouted from the housetops. It was seen and felt in the provisions made and the planning help offered to their customers.

Charley asked, "Is this the same size as the ships you mentioned in the office?"

"Yes. You're looking at a standard seventy-three foot trawler."

Below decks, Toady Lockwood crawled out of the shaft tunnel. No one knew what name Toady's mother had given him, and Toady wasn't telling. His initials were reported to be L.Z. Toady had discouraged one attempt in school to call him lazy by beating the idea out of the other's mind. Over time, the name Toady stuck, primarily as a result of his habit of sitting on his haunches. It stuck then, and it stuck now for the same reasons.

Toady was a little on the short side, made more apparent by his work partner, who stood almost six feet even, but his size didn't seem to limit Toady's ability. In fact, it made Toady more capable of some jobs they were called upon to do, such as crawling through the shaft tunnel to check the mid-point bearing for the propeller shaft. Normally, the steady rider could be inspected and adjustments made when the hold was empty by lifting he cover off the tunnel, but when they brought her back from her sea trials, someone thought she was ready to go and started to load stores for the delivery voyage.

Manuel Ruiz was sitting on the port engine beam, waiting for Toady to surface from under the hold where he had been adjusting the steady rider bearing, the mid-point support for the propeller drive shaft.

"Manny, think we got this one! There ain't a cup of water come through the packin' and the steady rider is about as true as we'll get her."

Toady took the offered cigarette, and squatted by the gearbox facing Manny. "Kick yer boots off and rest a bit, Toady. No sense in bustin' yer butt around here anymore. You hear about Jimmy Pearson this mornin'?"

A series of catastrophic visions flashed through Toady's mind as he said, "No, what happened?"

"They gave him notice this morning. Don't know if anyone else got it...maybe we'll find we're on the list when we go back on top!"

Toady relaxed, and realized he had tensed up with the thought of catastrophe. Then the weight of Manny's words sunk in.

"No shit? I couldn't believe it when they axed Tommy Lange last week. He hadn't been here that long, I guess, but no one could bitch about his work!" Toady paused, and then said, "You really think they'll cut down to us? I got eleven years here."

Toady jumped up, alarmed. "There's somebody come aboard."

"Relax. It's probably just the Mouse with our pink slips."

The Mouse was a frail looking, personable geriatric from the Personnel Department whom everyone kidded good naturedly as having handled the roster on the Ark. The Mouse reveled in the attention his nickname brought him.

Toady grumbled. "You're a lot of help." But he kept glancing nervously at the hatch above his head. He noticed, too, that Manny's bravado was waning quickly.

As they climbed aboard, Charley asked, "What's the beam?"

Dick answered, "It's about twenty feet amidships."

Charley was interested in how the Buick would ride on the aft deck, or more precisely, if it would fit there at all. If it wouldn't, arrangements would have to be made to ship the car, since it had been Charley's personal automobile and had already been sold to the Fisheries at a handsome profit.

It would be tight, but by removing some of the rigging, the car could possibly be hoisted over the side and laid lengthwise on the deck. They would place it as far aft as the space between the side rails and the fish hold hatch would permit and then replace the overhead rigging. Charley thought, *Bob can figure that one out.*

Standing behind the deckhouse looking aft, it seemed like there was lots of room. The area was about twenty by thirty feet with a five by eight foot hatch in the middle. This would shrink considerably when they strapped that seven-foot wide by eighteen-foot long station wagon in place. On the aft face of the deckhouse at the starboard edge was the hatch leading down to the engine room.

Bob, indicating the hatch with a sweep of his hand, asked, "Dick, may I?"

"Of course. You may find a couple of men down there trimming the shaft out. They'll be happy to answer any questions."

It was then that Bob's foot appeared through the hatch. The shoe told no story of what or who was violating their sanctuary, except that it wasn't a dockhand's shoe. But the fact that it was there meant its wearer had authority from the head shed, if not head shed material itself.

Both men jumped to their feet. They flipped their cigarettes into the bilge, but the pall of cigarette smoke hung like gossamer in the still air, mute testimony to their defiance of company rules. A cold sweat crawled down their backs. That telltale smoke could cost them their jobs. They may not have to wait long for that pink slip.

"Hello. Mind if I come down?"

The two men looked at each other. This one they had never seen before. "Nope," Manny said, "Come ahead."

"Thanks," Bob paused on the way down and looked around. It was clean as engine rooms go, but it wasn't the sparkling jewel seen from the dock. Nor did Bob expect it to be.

Bob's casual approach increased the wariness of the two workmen. They knew the people who were to pick up this ship, and this man certainly wasn't one of them.

The cigarette smoke hung on like an unwelcome guest. Even Manny's attempts to dispel it blowing out of the corner of his mouth only made it more noticeable by its movement.

"How does she look?" Bob asked.

"Well, we had a little whip in the shaft, "the tall one replied, "but we got her whupped. Far as we're concerned, she's ready to go."

"Would you mind if I asked a few questions?"

The two men's heart sank. Toady thought, *How am I going to tell my wife?*

When Bob explained they were interested in buying two boats, however, Toady's and Manny's spirits rose like rockets from the pit of despair to the `pinnacle of hope, all in the space of those three words: "Buying two boats." There was a kindred spirit borne in that instant. Here was hope. Here were friends!

"You're buying two boats?" Both men spoke almost in unison.

"Let's just say we need two boats. We're looking."

"Well," Manny said, "can we show you around? Do you have any questions? Just let us know how we can help! So you're looking for two boats. Well, you sure came to the right place."

The engine room deck was about eight feet below the main deck. Commanding this area forward of the ladder on the centerline was the yellow Caterpillar diesel. The engine room was blocked off aft by the forward bulkhead of the fish hold, and on each side by three gray fuel tanks leaving enough room on each side of the engine for a small man to pass comfortably. Bob wasn't small. Each of the fuel tanks had sight glass gages to indicate fuel quantity, which were interconnected by a system of plumbing lines and valves such that any tank or its sight glass could be isolated in the event of a rupture or leak.

Manny and Toady led Bob through the engine room, and forward through the forepeak storage bays. They showed him everything, explained everything. Bob knew he wouldn't remember all he was told. Manny and Toady didn't care...as long as he remembered THEM.

Bob thanked them both, and went topside through the forward hatch. He ambled back toward the aft deck, looking for Charley and Dick.

As he passed the deckhouse doorway, Dick called out, "Hi, Bob, we're in here! They were seated at the galley table. As Bob came in, Charley moved over in a somewhat futile attempt to make room. At twenty-six inches wide, the benches were designed for only one person. Bob sat down. Rather, half of him sat down. The other half defied gravity.

Charley said, "You were gone a long time. How were things below?"

"Just fine. The two men you had down there, Dick, were great. They really gave me first class treatment, covered the whole area below. I have a few questions, but they can wait for now."

"Good. It's going on five o'clock. I'd suggest we go back to my office now that you have a picture of a finished product, and figure out the next step."

Back in his office, Dick Bennett spread out the plans of the two boats under construction. They differed in fuel capacity and the design of the deckhouse. One had a twelve-foot wide deckhouse with a stepped wheelhouse; the other was the standard flat top wheelhouse version, only ten feet wide.

Dick said, "They only differ in the fuel capacity. The one with the smaller deckhouse carries 9400 gallons topped off, and he other carries 11,200 gallons.

Charley continued, "That should be plenty for an Atlantic crossing shouldn't it?"

"Should do that with about a week in reserve."

Charley continued the conversation, "Dick, how much do the buyers have in the boat we just saw?"

"Well, the base price was $120,000, but they had a lot of equipment on board that we didn't supply. So I can only guess, but I'd say it's about ten or twelve thousand over the base."

"That's $120," Charley mused, "subject to negotiation?"

"Well, uh, I don't know." Dick paused, then said, "You know, they say everything is negotiable, but I'll tell you, we really don't have a lot of room to move in as far as base price is concerned, but we could talk about what is to be included. We may have some latitude there."

"It's not that important right now. I just need to get some general numbers to work with. How soon could you have those next two boats ready?"

The direct questions regarding price caught Dick off guard. He was thankful to change the subject and give himself a little more time to plan his strategy. He needed desperately to sell those boats, but couldn't afford to lose money in the deal. And he didn't have an up-to-date breakdown of his costs, something accounting would have to jump on first thing in the morning. "I'm sorry, Charley, what was that?"

"I said, how soon could you have those two boats ready, assuming we had a Deal cut now?"

"OK. It will take us a month to finish them both, providing there are no options that would tie us up schedule-wise."

Charley said, "Let's look at options. I know the buyers want a sea water ice maker, which will require a 220-volt power source. I thought as long as we had to have 220 on board, we could eliminate the standard gas cook top along with the bottled gas storage. Do you see a problem there?"

"No," Dick replied, "the only problem might be in running the wiring on the 23 hull. The 35 hull is still open inside so even if the wire is strung, re-routing or re-sizing could still be done easily. But those icemakers. We don't get much call for those since most of our boats go out as freezer boats or ice boats. That is, they load their ice at the dock before sailing. They don't make it on the run, so I don't know a lot about your ice machine."

"I've been to the plant where these units are built and have some brochures which may help you, Dick. You are welcome to them."

For over an hour, they weighed the merits of the various options and the list continued to grow. It was topped off with the addition of two RV-type air conditioners, one to be mounted over the wheelhouse/captain's cabin, the other over the galley/crew's quarters.

"It's too late to get anything solid on this list today, but I will get someone working on it first thing tomorrow. Are you and Bob staying in town tonight? Or when can we get together again? I'd be pleased to take you to dinner."

Charley explained he was tied up with his family for the weekend. "You know, Dick, with this African thing, I haven't been home much. And I've cancelled a number of things we'd planned to do. Friday, that's tomorrow, isn't it? Friday they're flying to Orlando for a weekend at Disney World. The kids have been looking forward to that ever since I cancelled out on them the last time. That was in February! Said I'd make it up to them, so now they're calling me on it.""

Bob said, "Dick, there's a lot of equipment to price out here. Can you get it done tomorrow? It would seem early next week would make more sense, and if you ran into a problem, we could cover it by phone if it couldn't wait." They agreed, and Bob gave Dick one of his real estate cards.

"Thank you. You're right. I'll put a spec sheet together on the boats as we agreed, and price them out for, say, Tuesday? Give me a call Monday to confirm, OK?"

Dick dropped them at the airport and watched as they walked to the little Cessna 170B. What the airplane lacked in size, it made up in its condition. Dick's first thought as he looked at the machine was "It's made of mirrors!"

Actually, the airplane was polished every weekend that it was in Clearwater. Two high School boys with career aspirations in aviation did odd jobs at the Executive Airport to finance their dreams. Most of these tasks offered satisfaction only in monetary fashion, but the Cessna was different. It offered visible evidence of their dedication, which was not lost on other aircraft owners. It became their business card. More than that, this airplane became the signboard upon which the boys built a pretty good business. Although as far as the Cessna was concerned, their's was a labor of love, for which they were well paid.

Dick didn't know that. He didn't know who actually maintained the plane. He didn't know much about airplanes, period, but he appreciated a well-kept machine and this was certainly well kept. He knew boats, and had learned that those who cared for their boats, at least their workboats were usually hard working...and honest. He hoped that was the same with airplanes, too.

As they neared the plane, Charley asked, "Well, what do you think, Bob?"

"I think he has a lot more sunk into those boats than he's comfortable with, and was praying we would come by." Bob began his walk around inspection of the plane.

"You just won your milk shake. What else?"

"We can probably get a lot of those options buried in a sailaway price. In fact, he hesitated when you baited him. Now, you know when I was below decks on that trawler, in the engine room? There were two men working down there, trimming the shaft out, and we got to talking. Did you know Desco laid off seven men in the last month?"

"Really?"

"Really! OK, I'm ready if you are. Let's see what Jo has on the table tonight."

There wasn't much conversation on the way back to Clearwater, principally because it took super-powered lungs to compete with the roar of the engine and the rush of the wind. The Cessna was not built for executive comfort, but it did get into and out of small strips, sometimes necessary in Bob's commercial real estate pursuits. County roads had twice served as landing strips to visit with owners of potential development properties.

Charley was absorbed in the package of financial data and corporate historical information Dick had given him as they left the yard. Finally, Charley broke the silence. "Bob, I don't think we're going to do any better than Desco given the time constraints we're under unless it's in a used boat. They've got the product and it's here in your back yard. Let's concentrate on getting our best deal from them. We can call these other builders and have information packages sent to us as backup. That way, if we have to shift gears, we won't start out as totally unprepared as we did today. I think we got lucky!"

Charley left at noon for Orlando to pick up his fourth wife, Vickie, and their four-year-old son. For the boys, it was a normal Friday, with the added anticipation of final exams. Bob called Bender, whose eagerness approached that of Desco, but they had nothing on the shelf for sale. Lead time for the first boat from them would be four months.

Bob remembered Charley's words: "I think we got lucky", and thought, *Luck was Charley's middle name. It just couldn't all be skill, or could it? No, there's got to be a lot of luck mixed in there someplace.*

Dan returned from Florida State at 11:30 that night. Walt was up waiting for him, to fill him in on the happenings of the past few days. Dan interrupted Walt's tale, asking, "What's Charley paying, and how long is this job?"

"Well, we didn't talk about that, but I guess the job is about a month, until the boats are finished. Shoot, I'd work for almost nothing if I could learn how they built those boats."

"You always were a nut for boats. Don't get me wrong, I'm in. I just wanted to know how long we'd be working and how much I could save, because next year is going to be more expensive than this one at school. I filled out an application to manage an apartment complex, but hadn't heard anything before I left."

"Who is a nut about boats? I see you sailing off in the Cat every weekend you're home!"

"That was last weekend. The rest of the time you had the Cat. Anyway, forget it. I'm tired. We can talk about St. Augustine tomorrow."

The next morning over coffee, Charley said, "Bob, I appreciate what's been done, but there's a lot of work yet before we will see either of those ships head for Africa. Why don't we put you on retainer to outfit and crew them? I can't be here constantly, and I want someone I know and can trust to ride herd on whoever we buy from. You're here in Florida and we've known each other for a good long time." Charley inferred that he could not be comfortable with an unknown quantity. But Bob was thinking how much they could use the money after flushing all their savings down a legal rat hole.

"I'd like that," he said, "and I think the boys would like to get involved in it as well. School will be out in two weeks, so they would be available."

"You might let the word out in Tarpon Springs that we'll be needing a couple of experienced captains to work overseas. Who's that Greek fellow you know there?"

"That's Tacko Allisandratos. He would be a good one to turn stones over for us. He knows all the owners and captains on a first name basis, and can tell us who's good and who isn't."

"Now, I feel if I'm to be in Orlando by 1:30, I should probably leave here about eleven. Plus, I need to get a car. But first, we need to agree on a retainer, and some pocket money for the boys."

They worked out an acceptable monetary arrangement as far as Bob was concerned, and Bob felt the amounts Charley was offering the boys would be acceptable to them as well. This was instantly confirmed when Dan walked onto the patio and declared, "Whatever you're doing, count me in! If there's money involved, all the better."

"That's got to be one of your easiest negotiations, Charley!"

"You're right, Bob, but it isn't as satisfying to win one without a fight. When it falls in your lap, it makes you wonder how much you left on the table. But in this case ... Dan, did you mean you would go even if we weren't going to pay you?"

"Not if it is already offered. How much?" Everyone laughed.

Charley said, "I'll call you Sunday, Bob. Right now, I don't know if I'll come back here or meet you in St. Augustine Tuesday."

"The room is open, Charley, but why don't you call Monday afternoon instead, because we don't know yet if Bennett will have his numbers by Tuesday. In the meantime, I'll call Bender in Mobile Monday morning and see what they have used. Incidentally, Bender didn't have anything but new , and that would be for delivery four months down the pike. They're poking around their contacts in the Caribbean for used boats."

"OK, I'll call you Monday, and I'll plan on seeing you Tuesday, either here or in St. Augustine. Oh, Bob, you will probably have a visit from the Lloyd's of London people. They will be insuring he voyage and will probably want to make sure the ships are in good hands."

That weekend Bob visited the Public Library in Clearwater, checking out a copy of Chapman's *Seamanship*, a handbook of rules, regulations, and tips.

It was two weeks later after Charley had suggested Bob take one of the boats over to Ghana. On that day, many negative reasons began to churn around in Bob's mind, but the spirit of adventure was alive and well. So when Charley brought the boys into the picture, the spirit of adventure simply crushed Captain Negative and the whole world took on a different perspective. A short discussion with the boys settled everything, except how to break the news to Mom.

Charley Willis had an answer for that as well. The Government of Ghana, rather, the Bank of Ghana, would fly Jo and their daughter, Sandi, to Accra as part of the welcoming committee. No one questioned Charley's authority in making such an offer, and it didn't seem to change Jo's attitude toward the fact that her husband and possibly four sons were soon to be herded into a 73-foot, 98-ton wooden boat and disappear over the horizon. Perhaps forever.

"It's a chance of a lifetime, an opportunity the boys may never get again." "An education in itself...maturity...independence"...Bob never really knew when she accepted the fact that they were all going to jump aboard some "little dinghy" and leave her behind. Perhaps it was when Bob invited her along which, to her; was by far the least desirable choice.

"There are no signposts out there, are there?" she said. "Just how are you going to find Africa?"

"How about sailing east 'til you hit land?"

"Come on, be serious. Africa's a long way off."

"It will be easier than finding the Burbank airport on a smoggy day." The attempt at humor was lost; she was just not in the mood.

Bob argued, "After four years and all of our money, we're talking to Charley about working on a retainer basis to locate, outfit, and deliver two fishing vessels for the Government of Ghana. This tax thing has taken so much time, people think I'm out of the real estate business already. Maybe I am. Real estate has not been that steady lately and at 47, I'm too old to get back into the airline picture. So, when it comes down to the practical side of things, there really isn't much choice." Besides, when the boys understood what was happening, it became a contest where Jo was outnumbered four to one. Sandi stayed neutral. The boys saw to that.

In later years the elder Murrays learned some of the things the boys pulled off, with Sandi as an unwilling and uninvited witness. Through threat and coercion, they were able to keep their secrets. In fact, when the idea of her going to Africa with her mother to meet them got across, she jumped on the "go wagon".

So a greater challenge was born. No longer were they just doing a job, Bob and the boys were preparing their home for the next month or so. The menus were not for some unknown crewmen, they were their own. Consequently they did take an ample supply of steaks since they would have a seawater icemaker aboard for icing the fish down when the ship went into service. Seawater freezes between 28 and 29 degrees. The icemaker would be their frozen food locker for the voyage. And Bob called his eldest son in Idaho to tell him about the trip and invite him to come along. Steve said he would ask for time off, but he didn't think it was possible since he was assigned two jobs at Bunker Hill Mines in Kellogg, and that only for the past couple of months with no backups for either job. Steve was both the Plant Geologist and the Mine Safety Engineer. So Bob secretly kept his fingers crossed, but knew that given the same circumstances, he would have to do what was best for the company and his family. What was best for the company was also, in the long run, best for Steve as well. Steve had graduated from Washington State University in geology, and this is what he wanted as a career. They talked over the pros and cons and decided it was Steve's choice to go with his dream. Steve congratulated his parents on the news that they won their long battle with the IRS, which brought Bob back to the present

The next two weeks proved to be the coup de grace to Steve's possibility of joining the crew. Two Bureau of Mines inspectors, Larry Weinberg and Eddie Adams, dropped in unannounced for an inspection of the Bunker Hill facility. This inspection required that they go underground, but no further than was necessary to determine that applicable safety policies were implemented and were being observed and proper equipment was on hand and available. The mine had an entrance level on an elevation about the same as the main street of Kellogg. From the entrance, the tracks for the ore cars continued level to the headworks for the inclined shafts accessing both the upper and lower levels. The three men, joined at the entrance by Will Beach, shift foreman, decided to go up to the no.7 level, two levels above them and work their way back to the entrance. After inspecting the no.7 level and the air handling and communications systems on no.7, they dropped down to the no.9 level. They determined that a visit to production areas on the no.9 level would be all they would need for that day. So the four of them set out for the no.9 level, as sufficient for their inspection that day. The no.9 level was producing ore out of side drifts. It was unusually, almost eerily, quiet in the mine. Will asked, "What time is it?"

"It's about 1:15."

Steve explained, "The last blast is set for 2:15, so the next shift will have fresh material to work on."

The group trudged to one of the stopes [a horizontal excavation used to pursue an ore vein (in mining)] where ore was being withdrawn , with Steve and Eddie in the lead, followed by Will and Larry. As they entered the stope, Will elbowed his way past Eddie and Steve, and was in the front of the group when the 14 second blast sequence went off. The purpose of the delay in the sequence and the location of the charges **was** to move as much material as possible to the far wall of the access tunnel using the force of the blast to help break the rock down into more manageable sizes, where this material passes through a grate to a hopper on the floor below to feed the ore carts. It is then transported by ore train to the outside. With that much rock coming out of the stope, and of that size, it's amazing that more serious injuries did not occur. The injuries that did occur were serious enough, however. In addition to cuts and bruises, Steve, Eddie and Will suffered hearing impairments. Will Beach suffered by far most of the injuries. A rock deprived him of sight in his left eye, and another large rock struck him in the jaw shattering it and stripping his flesh away from his neck as skillfully as a surgeon with scalpel and sponge exposing the carotid artery, which was oozing a little blood. Steve prayed that the carotid would not rupture. The heart's beating could be seen in the pulsation of the carotid. Both of Will's ankles were mangled, and the flesh stripped off his left arm down to the bone from the elbow to the wrist with equal surgical skill. Their hardhats prevented any other head injuries except hearing loss. Steve sent Eddie out to the emergency phone, to have the traffic coordinator stop all inbound/outbound traffic to the no.9 level, except to send an empty ore cart to transport the injured. Eddie hopped one of the exiting trains to advise those on top what had happened. At once, Steve commandeered all loose items of clothing from everyone, including shirts, tee shirts and any other available outerwear to bind up Will's wounds. When Eddie arrived outside several mine employees intercepted him, and when they sent the evacuation train in to get the injured, it was well populated with workmen coming in to aid in the rescue.

The other inspector, Larry Weinberg, assisted Steve as they waited for the ambulance and assisted the paramedics when they arrived. When Steve emerged from the mine, he was wearing only his boots, socks, his B.V.D. shorts, and a nylon jacket. The quick work of that group got the injured to the ambulance and en route to the hospital in less than twenty minutes, and saved Will Beach's life. (Will won't ever make a full recovery, but considering the nature of his injuries, his recovery is nevertheless miraculous.) Larry, Eddie, and Steve were treated and released at the hospital.

The initial investigation lasted more than two months. Steve was absolved of any blame because the investigation showed written procedures existed and were not followed, which could have prevented the whole incident. The bottom line, however, meant that Steve was to remain at Kellogg as a witness for the company in the disciplinary action taken against those responsible for failure to follow set emergency procedures involving revised blast schedules.

When Bob learned of the Bunker Hill disaster and the length of time the investigation was estimated to take .he figured they had best not count on Steve. The crewing had been figured on a five-man basis, so Bob and the boys sat down to discuss the problem. Dan suggested they contact Jimmy White, a classmate of his at Florida State University. Jimmy was well known to Bob and Jo. The Whites were long-time friends of the Murrays, and Bob figured Jimmy would make a good balance for all the Murrays running loose.

There was another decided advantage to the program for the Murrays. Each month, the retainer would continue to be deposited to their account and living expenses would be minimal.

The idea of unfavorable odds never seemed to faze Jo Murray before with Bob flying so much, and she wasn't wilting at the pressure the men in the family were able to muster now, but when Sandi jumped on board, Jo withdrew any open resistance to the venture and subconsciously resigned herself to widowhood.

The vessels were acquired and were being outfitted, a job the three boys delighted in. Bob had interviewed two experienced fishing captains from Key West; one of them was to arrive in St. Augustine the following week. Meantime, at Desco that week a workman came running out to the ships, now both in the water, calling, "Cap'n.Murray , Cap'n Murray!"

Bob stuck his head out of the galley area on board one of the Alphas, saying, "I'm over here. What do you need?"

"There's a couple men in he office to see you. Mr.Bennett sent me to find you."

"Thank you, I'll be right there!"

The two men introduced themselves as investigative agents from Lloyd's of London, and were there to investigate Bob Murray's qualifications to drive one of

Lloyd's insured vessels to Ghana. They had quite a dossier on Bob already, so they limited their questioning to light signal displays while underway, subjects like the number of mast lights to be displayed while towing or under tow by another vessel, the light displays while at anchor, and the like. Bob was still unaware of Charley's intention to designate him as Master of the Voyage. He wouldn't learn that until the closing papers were signed and the Alpha Boats were on their way.

Rick and Dan were married and Walt was a shaky single. Everything had been planned around a five-man crew, so Dan suggested they invite a friend of the Murray family, one of his classmates at Florida State University, Jimmy White, to join the party. Jimmy White would be a welcome addition to the party, a means of diffusing some of the competition that is almost always present when siblings get together without other activities to entertain . So they held a meeting, just the three boys and Bob regarding Jimmy since Steve could not come. It was a unanimous decision. Jimmy was in, if he could make it.

As the date of departure approached, Captain Joe Shell joined the group, followed by Captain Dave Banks. Joe had been Master of a 210-foot Oceanographic Survey vessel and Dave Banks sailed the Seven Seas for 30 years. Both men had outstanding reputations in the ocean fishing trade. They were a study in opposites, however.

Joe was a quiet, studied man who spoke little and said much. It paid to listen. Dave spoke much, and if you listened carefully, you found he said much as well. But, you had to pick the lessons out of the seaweed. Joe was short, Dave was not. Joe could have passed as an accountant or a banker. In Dave, you saw salt in the hair and the eyebrows. It was obvious he'd knocked around the world a few times and took direction from points of the compass. He didn't have a right and left hand – he had starboard and port everything.

Joe and Bob handled the final planning for the voyage, figuring to sail down the Florida coast across the north coast of Cuba and Hispanola, and then putting in to San Juan to fuel and stretch the legs. For crews they had four boys, two experienced captains and Bob. They also had four Ghanians that the Government of Ghana sent over, who were supposed to be made into sailors by the time they got back to Ghana. These men would be sailing with Dave and Joe when the ships went to work in Africa, but they didn't know much about modern ships and fishing methods. Fishing in Ghana was primarily done from overgrown, overloaded canoes that when loaded had very little freeboard.

Joe said, "I think we should keep the natives together, but will have to have one of us on watch all the time until we're sure they can hack it on their own."

Bob agreed. "I want to use Rick as a first mate. I think he should sail with you to Puerto Rico. He could learn a great deal about the equipment and handling from you. Banks could run with me and cover a lot of the same ground during that run. That should give us about five or six days together, providing Banks can stand me that long."

Joe replied, "Yeah, it'll take us about five days if the weather holds. We'll do a little better than 9 knots."

Bob said, "Charley was right. He told me it would be a little slower than flying! During that time, Bob gave a lot of thought to what it would mean to have that time with the boys. There was much that could be accomplished without the distractions that are such a common occurrence in daily lives. Two of the more common tools in carving character would be evident, he thought, available in this trip - they are survival and self preservation!

Dan appointed himself a committee of one to contact Jimmy. Jimmy White was of an adventurous spirit, one that fit very well into that of the rest of the crew on Alpha II. He had tentatively agreed to join the group on this voyage, but only with his father's blessing. When his father, D.C. White, found out that the Bob was going to be Captain of the ship Jimmy would be on, he gave his blessing to the adventure. D.C. and his wife, Lucille, both realtors in Tallahassee, Florida, took a day off several days before the Alpha II was set to sail and drove Jimmy to St. Augustine. Jimmy unloaded his personal items at the Desco Yard and Dan, Walt, and Rick started on a crash course to bring Jimmy up to speed. They broke for a quick lunch - the Murrays and the Whites. Then it was back to stowing Jimmy's things and the non-perishable stores. No one was really sure Lucille White was ever convinced of the wisdom that prompted this foolishness, but she let Jimmy go!

Those last days in June 1975 seemed to move faster and faster. To a point, it was like the noisy, uphill climb on a roller coaster. There was time to look around, to think, to enjoy the view. In the back of your mind, however, you knew things were going to change.

Change they did! In mid June, the ride began! Anticipation of problems came more by luck than any skill or knowledge of Bob or the boys or the two captains accompanying on the other boat. Material delays, the endless lists of things required, not only for the voyage to Africa, but for the start of fishing operations once the ships arrived, and the learning process all contrived to trash their best laid plans. Like the roller coaster, it seemed the best one could do was hang on! Sea trials were finally run on the St. John River and did reveal some minor repairs and adjustments, and, of course, there were two ships to check out.[] **T**he St. John**s** was not the ideal place for sea trials. You could not open the throttle for fear of washing docks and underpinnings out along the banks of the river, provoking the ire of the waterfront residents. Insurance documents, purchase and sale documents, coast guard documents...reminded Bob of his days at Boeing. The saying was: "When the weight of the paper equals the design gross of the airplane, we'll fly it." Bob felt there was certainly a similar witticism relating to ships of the sea.

Joe, Bob, and Rick made a final shopping trip to Jacksonville to get up-to-date charts and the *Coastal Pilot for the West Coast of Africa*, a publication that lists landmarks, radio aids, and other information vital to a seaman navigating in those waters. Joe was aware of Charley's desire to bring a load of fish in the first time they docked in Tema, but was wary of their ability to accomplish this feat. The charts they found did not change that feeling.

Reviewing the charts, Joe said, "These show a wide sandy plain that should be pretty good for a sweep, but we'd have to be lucky to find a good catch with no more information to go on than this."

"Where can we get what we need?"

"Unfortunately," Joe said, "the best is the fishermen that fish those waters. It would be ideal if we could talk to them before we try it ourselves. They could save us a lot of time."

"That won't be possible. Charley wants fish in the hold when we dock the first time. How about your crew? Do they have any fishing experience in that area?"

"They don't have any real fishing experience, period! The closest they come is some limited experience crewing coastal steamers. Two of them with fishing experience are limited to the coastal canoes, and they don't know where they were fishing when they found productive areas. The captain (or boat owner) would call out something like, 'nets', or maybe it was, 'nuts', so they would cast their nets over the side. No, we're going to be on our own over there!"

Bob asked, "What would be wrong with running a pattern over the area scanning with the fish finder? We don't have to fill the hold, just get enough aboard for a dog and pony show."

"Yeah, we could run a pattern. But I'd be more interested in getting a good paint of the bottom to see what kind of hang-ups we would be dragging through. Coral outcroppings, or old wrecks can be hazardous to your health. With 360-horsepower working at the end of a 30-foot outrigger, a hangup can heel your boat and flip you over before you can set your coffee cup down!"

"Won't these Furunos give us a good paint of the bottom?" Then Joe outlined some of the dangers encountered in trawler operations. It would be hard to explain to Yeboah how one of his ships could sink just 10 miles from its destination, particularly after having navigated 5800 miles of ocean.

On the morning of the proposed departure, an army of people invaded the shipyard and overran the boats. Charley was leading a contingent from Ghana, insurance people, politicians, and the staff from the shipbuilding company. The Desco management staff threw a going away or "getting out their hair" party.

THE SAILAWAY INSPECTION TEAM : L-R: **Bob Murray; Charley Willis; Bertram Amin; Mr. Butto**, Mgg Dir, Bank of Ghana, **P. Yeboah**, Mgg Dir, Ag Devel Bank, Ghana; **Dick Bennet**, Desco.

Visiting firemen were all over the lead ship, the *Alpha II*, loaded with questions. They wanted to play with the radios, start the engines, and see the icemaker work. The crews wanted to get out of there. On top of this, the morning departure brought the delivery of supplies ordered for the voyage. Frozen foods, for example, were left to the last, since the icemaker could not be operated in port. The water in port was too contaminated to pack food in, even in a frozen state.

MORE INSPECTION TEAM : L-R: **Dick Bennett**; **Bert Amin**; **P. Yeboah**; **P. Yeboah**; **M. Butto**; **Charley Willis**, Unknown Desco.

Charley called Bob aside.

"Bob, here are your ship's papers and $2000 in hard cash as a captain's fund. And here are the papers for Alpha I. Please see that Joe gets his before you sail."

Charley shuffled through more papers. He smiled and held up another document. "Here is a credit document from Texaco for fuel. Your fuel has been prepaid in Ghana and the Texaco people in San Juan are expecting you, but if you put in anywhere else, look up the Texaco people. They will probably be your best friends there."

Until the time they sailed, the retainer due Bob had been dutifully deposited in his bank, together with the expense check to cover the many trips to St. Augustine and the numerous items paid for by cash. The order of the day was, "Not to worry!"

Joe and Rick got off easy. The crowds were on the *Alpha II*. Joe sat in his wheelhouse and smiled. He had four Ghanaians to stow his last minute supplies, and no one to trip over. The *Alpha II* crew had no place to hide.

Bob finally made his way to the Alpha I. "Joe, here is your copy of the ship's papers. The original sale documents will be signed beyond the territorial limits and will go back to Ghana with the bank people. These release papers should cover us if we have to put in anywhere other than Puerto Rico. Charley has also given us money to cover fuel and supplies in San Juan, and we have an open line of credit with Texaco for fuel in San Juan. I have the documents to cover that."

The gulls overhead seemed restless. Their incessant screeching did seem to blend with the cacophony of sounds floating over the river. Joe had seen this all before, including the increased activity on the part of the gulls when a sailing is imminent. So had Bob, when he took the visiting airline personnel out in the Sea Esta fishing for red snapper and grouper in the Gulf. Or maybe it was Joe's imagination, but he could recall numerous times when he stood on deck contemplating a voyage, that these timeless creatures would pay their farewell with their noisy serenade. One landed on the forward rail, eyeing Joe and Bob, perhaps anticipating a reward for their symphony.

Bob studied the bird for a moment, then squinted into the lowering sun and remarked, "Joe, no one has told us yet that the closing documents are done, and frankly, by the time Ghanaians get through playing with all the toys on board, it's going to be a pretty late start."

"Yeah, particularly with a new ship that's only had a few hours trial run on the river. I'd rather see us shove off in the morning."
"I'd feel better about that, too. I can take the boys back to the hotel, but your crew will have to stay on board. I don't want to be responsible for them wandering around in St. Augustine or Jacksonville tonight, or for that matter, trying to find them in the morning."

The native crewmen had come aboard the previous day. They had come in with the officials from the Bank of Ghana and from the Ghana government, and had worked hard loading Joe's ship. Joe was gaining a respect for them but no one had any idea as to their personal habits, particularly regarding drinking. On board, that would not be a problem.

Joe replied, "Dave Banks can sack out on your ship, he's going to be there en route to San Juan anyway. I'll stay here with the Ghanaians.

"OK. Let's see if we can split Charley away from that group long enough to set up for tomorrow morning."

The ships were docked in tandem, with *Alpha I* astern of *Alpha II*. It happened that Charley was pointing something out on Joe's ship to Mr. Yeboah of the Agricultural Bank, the actual purchasers of the two vessels. Bob caught Charley's eye, and the three men met on the dock.

"Charley, it's going to be too late to get underway tonight," Bob offered, "particularly since your party doesn't show any signs of breaking up."

"If you want them off the ship, just say the word. They want these vessels in Ghana as soon as possible. The government there is paying about twenty million U.S. dollars a year to Senegal to fish Ghanian waters for them."

Joe said, "The problem is running an unknown ship after dark on its first full-fledged proving run. We'd like to get to know in the daylight how well they built them. If there's going to be any surprises, they will probably show up in the first few hours at sea."

Charley said, "Bob, what are you fellows suggesting?"

"We'd like to see the closing set for tomorrow morning instead of this afternoon. That way, once the documents are signed we can turn south and run. If it has to be today, then we'd suggest we come back into port for the night and get an early start tomorrow."

"That makes sense. Let me talk to Yeboah and the Desco people, and I'll get back to you."

Charley turned back to the *Alpha II.* Bob watched him step aboard and said, "We'll leave tomorrow. Charley has a way of getting what he wants."

"If that's the case, we have to do something about the frozen stuff we put on board."

"Yeah. We could have Desco ice it down for tonight, or...or if they have any insulated blankets here, we could borrow them for the night. I've got all that equipment in the hold, sitting right under the hatch. Could be a problem getting ice up to the forward corner, and if that stuff is covered, it shouldn't melt."

Rick and Walt had joined the two men on the dock and were put to work protecting the frozen food. Their fires of incentive were lit when Bob mentioned, "I sure don't want to throw this river water on stuff I'm going to eat, frozen or not!"

The closing was rescheduled for ten o'clock the next morning, June 27, 1975. Banks and Joe stayed on board the two boats since all the stores were now aboard. Little provision had been made to safeguard the stores after they were boarded, since second story burglaries are rare occurrences at sea. Also, the Ghanaians were restricted by US Immigration and Naturalization Service (INS) to remain on their ship unless they possessed written authorization from the captain to go ashore. They were allowed entry into the States only as shipboard crew. That meant the captain of their vessel held the ultimate responsibility for them in the eyes of the US INS. Neither Joe, Bob, nor Dave Banks felt easy about turning these men loose in a strange land, particularly when they could be held responsible for their actions.

About four o'clock that afternoon, everything returned from its aggravated state of confusion to the state of normalcy with which everyone was more familiar.

So Bob and the boys returned to the Thunderbird Hotel, taking a change of clothing and a toothbrush. Later that evening they gathered for what was to be their last dinner at a fully stationary table for a long time. The coffee stayed in the cup until you drank it. The saltshaker did not pass itself around the table. The next morning real eggs and bacon graced the table.

None of the boys needed an alarm clock the next morning. Jimmy White was the first one up and his exuberance was infectious - instantly infectious!

Dan and Walt had been immersed in that deep kind of sleep, totally oblivious to anything and everything around them. They had been, that is, until Jimmy poured a glass of cold water in their faces!

The romp was on! Jimmy was no match for the two of them, so in short order he was soaked to the teeth. So was the room.

Rick and Bob had stayed in an adjoining room. The commotion awakened Rick, whose first thought was to get out of there, that an emergency existed. As the voices increased, Rick recognized them and thought the other boys were in trouble. Bob was awake now, too, and had figured out what was going on. Slipping on his pants, he padded barefoot to the boys room and pounded on the door. "Hey! What's going on in there?"

Silence.

It was like a spring-loaded water faucet snapped from full flow to shut. Inside the room, the silence was deafening. Until Dan snickered. Then Jimmy laughed and Walt went after him again.

Bob had noticed the silence and thought someone was coming to open the door. When the action started again, Bob pounded again. More silence.

"Who is it? Came a feeble voice from behind the door.

"I want to know what's going on in there!"

"It's your dad," Jimmy whispered, and started kicking anything loose out of sight under the bed. Walt joined him, and Dan headed for the door, looking over his shoulder. When he was sure most of the devastation was out of sight, he opened the door a crack.

"Oh, it's you!" Dan tried his best to feign surprise.

"Don't give me that crap," Bob said, acting irritated and upset. But the excitement of the adventure ahead invaded his psyche and all he could manage was, "What's going on in here?" Before anyone could answer, a chuckle escaped him.

Dan smiled. Walt smiled. Jimmy, who didn't know the darker side of Bob, held back any outward show, but looking at Dan and Walt, felt it was OK to smile too.

Rick appeared in the doorway. The scene opened before him... "That's a pretty wild alarm clock you guys have!" That broke the tension, and everyone laughed. "Please don't bring it on board with you!"

Bob said, "Listen, we do have to keep it down, or we'll have to stay on board tonight." Everyone laughed again. "Now, let's get this room in a little better shape, and....Jimmy, what happened to you?" Bob had been surveying the room since he came in and just now realized Jimmy could have taken first prize in a wet T-shirt Contest.

"Well, Mr. Murray, there were these two guys...." More laughter.

Dan was not one to let the blame stop there, saying, "Jimmy dumped water – cold water – on us while we were sleeping."

To which Bob said, "What did you do to instigate that response? Well, never mind, get this room in better shape so we can get out of here without a police escort."

"OK, that's over now. Let's get our gear together, get some breakfast and take off. I'd like to be back at the yard around 7:30."

As they left the rooms, the second floor walkway offered a panoramic view of a scene only a master painter could have conceived. The early rain had scrubbed the day behind its ears, brightening every color. Patches of the early sunlight filtered through the trees. White butterflies danced in the sunlight, joined occasionally by some of solid yellow. The grass was sprinkled with diamonds and the birds in the trees sang their appreciation of the beauty laid before them.

It was like an omen. The small group of travelers stopped on the walkway, taking in the scene. Bob said, "It looks like we have a good day to start with. Let's hope it stays this way the whole trip."

Rick asked, "What's the chance of that happening?"

"Not very good. This is the beginning of the hurricane season, and we're heading toward the area where they spawn." If there was any danger implied by the thought of bad weather, it was lost on the whole of the group. Adventure lay at their doorstep, and they were eager to enter.

The sale documents and money exchange was to be consummated at ten o'clock beyond the Continental Limits in international waters for tax purposes. At seven the group of boys had a last cup of coffee and headed to the shipyard. At the time, they didn't realize how really good that cup of coffee was!

There wasn't much to be done aboard the ship, since they had been prepared to sail the previous day, but a re-check was in order. So each one was assigned an area of their ship to check, and Dave Banks coordinated the overall effort on the Alpha II. Joe and Rick went through a similar exercise on the Alpha I, except that the two of them re-checked the whole ship with the Ghanaian crew in tow. Joe didn't believe the Ghanaian crew had been aboard long enough to become familiar with the ship and all its equipment. Joe had made his living in part with ships for many years and Rick had watched this one grow from the keel up.

Alpha I had been set up to trawl for fish on the way in to Tema, so there was no outward appearance that this ship was not going out for a week offshore in the fishing grounds.

Alpha II was different. The most notable difference was the Buick Station Wagon loaded on the aft deck. The ship had a beam of twenty feet, which just accommodated the car setting fore and aft about eight feet forward of the aft rail. The car had been loaded with office and personal supplies for those who would be remaining in Ghana. It was secured to the deck, and then wrapped in two layers of clear plastic held in place with prodigious amounts of duct tape. Finally a tarpaulin was lashed down on top of all this. *Alpha II* looked like it carried a five-inch gun turret on the aft deck, without the guns.

The plan was that as the ships approached Ghana, Joe and Dave were to drop their nets and take aboard fish, shrimp, and anything else left lurking in those waters, to impress the local reception committee. Dave Banks was opting for mermaids. He was always opting for mermaids!

Joe agreed to the exercise, but both Joe and Bob had reservations. They worked out a program where Joe and Dave could come with fish, but with a minimum of danger.

Bob recalled Joe's explanation , "Trawling in unknown waters can be hazardous to your health, particularly if there are underwater coral outcroppings or uncharted wrecks that could hang your net. At four knots trawl speed, with roughly three hundred fifty horsepower working at the end of your outriggers a hang-up can heel the ship and flip it over before you can set your coffee cup down." They had no working charts that showed minor obstructions or known areas where fish schooled in the Ghana area.

As ten o'clock approached, excitement mounted. The closer the clock crawled up on ten, the more there was to do. So the increasing excitement served to heighten energy, activity, and anticipation. Another "official" visit before they sailed by the government and bank representatives accompanied by Charley proved to be a stabilizing influence. This time, they were more interested in the route, estimated times, and planned communications procedures. The party was over. This time it was all business.

L-R: **Unidentified, Ghana Ministry of Ag Official, P. Yeboah (dark suit), Charley Willis (white shirt & tie), Bertram Amin, Ghana government official.**

chapter eight

SAILAWAY TO SAN JUAN

There was nothing for the crews on board the Alpha Boats to do at the actual closing except to wait the few minutes it took for the sale documents to be signed by all parties and for the insurance to be validated with the Agricultural Development Bank of Ghana as loss payee. Until the closing, insurance was Desco's responsibility. Lloyd's of London was the lead underwriter for the Agricultural Development Bank.

Charley had named Bob as Master of the Voyage in the application for the delivery voyage insurance endorsement. He showed Bob the insurance documents during the morning visit. That was the first Bob knew about being responsible for the delivery!

Command is not the proper word. There was only one time, late in the voyage, when Bob and Joe did not agree on a course of action. If there was any disappointment, irritation, or other emotion on Joe's part, it didn't show. Neither at the beginning of the trip, nor at the end, nor at any point in between.

No, the word should be cooperation. There was cooperation between the boats, between the crews on each boat, and certainly between Joe and Bob.

"Walt, go below and give them fuel tanks a good lookin' over. Partic'ly around the tops. Yestiddy's the fust time they been full, an' we don't want a loose fittin' or a bad weld sloshin' fuel around our insides when we get underway."

"Yessir, Captain Dave,", Walt replied.

Jimmy White said, "I'll go with you. You check one side and I'll check the other. Then we can swap sides and check each other."

"Good thinking, Jimmy!"

When they came up topside, they found the show was about to get on the road. Charley and the others had boarded the Bertram cabin cruiser that would serve as the boardroom. Aboard *Alpha II*, Banks was standing by the forward line, Dan was by the aft line. Walt was on the spring line, a line running from the dock about mid-ships to a cleat aft. This line works as a fulcrum allowing the helmsman greater maneuverability at the dock, particularly when room to maneuver is limited by other vessels tied close in on the bow and on the stern.

"Cast off forward!"

Dave Banks loosed the lines. "Cast off aft. Hold on the spring line!"

Bob slipped the gears into forward, the spring line tightened, and swung the bow into the river just enough to clear the vessel ahead. As Alpha II came clear, Bob eased the boat into the river, straightened the rudder and stabilized the turns on the engine at 800 RPM. The spring line slacked off.

"Cast off the spring line!" he called.

Walt loosed the lines, and stowed them, coiled, then came back to the wheelhouse.

They were underway!!

Bob set the turns for 1000 as they cleared the dock area. Dave Banks reached over and gave a sharp salute with the horn, which Desco people returned with waves, smiles, and cheers! Banks took it in stride, but that little response filled each of the others with pride, with a sense that they had done a good job, and were actually appreciated. There were times when each of them questioned that point, when they felt they were more in the way than a help. The closer they came to sail away, the less that feeling overtook them. Each of them realized they were going to make their target date, and that it would never have happened if they were not part of the team. The cheers were both acknowledgement and reward enough.

Walt was still waving when he glanced back through the open hatch to see Rick and Joe ease into the river behind them. "They're clear", he announced. "Here they come."

Also joining the entourage was an armada of gulls, a raucous bunch of feathered well-wishers that had no trouble in making their presence known. Once out of sight of the Desco yard, the euphoria that lifted the neophyte sailors to their present emotional heights slipped gradually toward quiet resignation. When they had this ship out before, it was a known fact that they would be back in two or three hours. Today was different, a difference you could feel. It was happening! The gulls let them know it!

It seemed the gulls' excitement rose when a boat headed downstream. Banks said, "I'll swear these damn birds smell fish before you catch them. It's this way every time you take a boat out or bring one in. Once we were coming back in and a bunch of these things was crowding around the aft end, so one of the folks I had on board took two herring and tied them together with about four or five feet of fish line. Then he threw the bait in the air. You know, two of those birds grabbed those herring and started to fly off. Of course, the other birds were still tryin' to place a claim on those herring, so these two are dodgin' and jukin'. They got maybe twenty feet when their dodgin' and jukin' sent them in different directions. When they ran out of line, their heads snapped around and one of them lost his herring. But another one grabbed it and the whole show was replayed. Last thing I seen was a gull with an empty string hanging' out of his craw."

"Where was this?"

"That was a long time ago. I had taken a sport fishin' group out of Key West, and they was in pretty good spirits. We'd had a good day."

The Bertram was better than 500 yards ahead, disappearing occasionally around a bend in the river.

"Dave, it looks like the Bert is pulling away. Should we jack the engine up a little?"

"Naw, they ain't goin' anywhere, Bob. They'll slow down when they get to the bar and hit open water. We're pushin' too much water in here to go much faster without washin' in the banks and damagin' docks 'n things with our wake makin' everyone mad at us."

Dave's comment drew everyone's attention to the scenery slipping past them. They were just passing a small mangrove thicket, well populated with egrets and ibis. A blue crane was stalking its prey in the shallows with that slow, herky-jerky one-foot-at-a-time movement, then in the snap of a finger, he speared a small fish with his beak, flipped it into the air, and caught it on its way down.

As the thicket passed behind, Dave said, "You know, it's about coffee time. Why don't one of you boys try your hand at coffee buildin'? You know it takes both caffeine and diesel to make one of these things go, don't you?"

If eagerness was an asset, the boys would be millionaires. They dashed for the hatch, Jimmy in the lead. In the galley, however, there was no pushing, each one mentally dividing the project into its elements, pitching in to do what wasn't being done. Had Dave seen the effort in the galley, he would have re-stated his next comment.

"Looks like you're going to have your hands full just keepin' 'em on board, Bob. Better to have 'em wantin' to do something than just sittin' on their duff, I guess. But I'd sure make sure they don't get to horsin' around while we're underway."

"I'm not too concerned, Dave. I've watched them work together for the past four weeks, but we do need some rules to cover safety items. I'll scribble some down – you can look them over and add whatever you think is best."

"I ain't much for written stuff, it don't seem to stay around long. But we've got four or five days to work with them, and I'm certain we can pound something into them that would last a while."

On the way forward, Dan let out a shriek, "Lookit! Up there on the bridge!" He started dancing and hopping around on the bow, pointing up at the St. John's bridge. Their eyes following his direction, they finally saw what Dan saw. Bobi and Debi were on the bridge, waving goodbye, perhaps forever! Bob gave them a long salute on the horn. Bob found out later that Debi's father had told her that this was foolishness, it would be a miracle if she ever saw them alive again.

On *Alpha I*, Rick had seen the antics of Dan, and the objects of his attention. It took a little time, but when he realized it was his wife on the bridge, Rick stuck his head in the wheelhouse and had Joe give the two girls a long blast on the horn. The two ships slipped proudly under the bridge with the boys scurrying back to the aft rail watching until there was nothing more to watch for.

The excitement over, the coffee came. Walt had fashioned a tray out of a cardboard box, and proudly carried four cups of hot coffee to the wheelhouse. "One dose of caffeine apiece. Jimmy didn't want any yet."

"Thank you, Walt, Dan." Bob took a cup and sipped the hot liquid. Banks did the same.

Bob stared into the cup. "Where did you guys get the coffee? From the medicine chest?"

Dan said, "We know. Walt and I both drank some before we came up here, and agreed it doesn't taste homemade. But we don't know what's wrong with it."

"It tastes like something you'd soak your feet in to kill fungus."

"You got that right, Bob," Banks said. "Here, you take her. I'm going to check something."

Dave returned a few minutes later with a glass of water in his hand. "Here, take a sip of this," offering the glass to Bob. Bob took a sip and almost gagged.

Walt asked, "What's that?"

"That," Dave said, "is our water. When they install these lazarette tanks, they dump a lot of disinfectant in them and are supposed to run it through the pipes, and then flush it out. Friends, we wasn't flushed out! In fact I'm not sure they even tried to get the disinfectant out!"

"Is there only one tank?"

"Yep, Dan, we have 900 gallons of well-treated water. Makes lousy coffee, but it won't kill you. Besides, you drink coffee for the caffeine, not the water." Dave's analysis did nothing to brighten the spirits of the crew that day. There were five, maybe six days to good water.

Jimmy started singing "Cool Water". Soon the rest joined in, and the water problem was relegated to a nuisance item, one that was not going to spoil the voyage.

Dave Banks reached up and grabbed the VHF microphone. He could see Alpha I chugging along like an obedient puppy, some one hundred yards astern. "*Alpha II* to *Alpha I*, Hey Joe, you there?"

"Yeah, Dave, Go ahead."

"You tried your water yet?"

"No. Why?"

"You go ahead and try it. If you don't have any answers then, then I'll tell you."

"OK. Rick's going back to take a look."

As the *Alpha II* rounded the headland, they could see the Bertram plowing into the onshore swells. It pitched and bobbed in the six-foot swells outside the bar, like a cork in a washing machine. Bob wondered how many of the bankers aboard had sea legs. "If the Bertram keeps that up much longer, I'll bet some of those bankers would be lining up to swim for shore."

"Yeah," Dave answered, "that's the problem with a smaller boat, going through the breakers. We got an advantage with our weight and size. But it really ain't as bad as it looks from here, and they're already through the worst part. See the line he's takin'? Just follow him. We ain't goin' to get bucked around nearly as much as they did. And you can kick the turns up to fifteen hundred."

Bob set the throttle for fifteen hundred and felt the ship ease ahead, becoming more stable. At ninety tons loaded, eighty-some-odd tons as she sat now, the *Alpha II* was not going to "jump" anywhere. But with the little increase in speed, the side-to-side rocking motion was better controlled, and the increase in stability was apparent.

Banks was right. When the *Alpha II* reached the bar, she plowed ahead as though the waves were an aggravation, a nuisance to be tolerated, even though each wave was felt in the sudden perceptible slowing of the boat. There was little pitching motion. It was like the trawler lowered its shoulder and blasted the wave. These waves were not large enough to come over the bow, but they did cast a lot of spray to the side.

To no one in particular Bob said, "She's like a bulldozer going through these breakers, isn't she?"

Banks replied, "Well, she's got a Caterpillar engine, don't she?"

During the signing, they held their position about fifty yards from the Bertram. The documents took longer than they had expected, but finally, they got a blast from the Bertram's horn and Charley came out on the aft deck to wish a good trip. We returned the salute with two short blasts on our horn, ran the turns up to 1800 and turned to 148 degrees They were on their own! Africa, look out!

That first day was spent in shaking down the boat. The river trials did not give them much opportunity to check everything, for in the St. Johns, they could not get the engine up to speed or their wake would have done a lot of damage along the riverbank. So, this became the real shakedown. Surprisingly, everything started out 'in the green' as far as equipment went. Banks did yeoman's duty checking both topside and below decks, with Walt following his every move like a puppy learning to heel.

About an hour out, Banks was on the after deck, and called, "Bob, come over here, I want to show you something we missed." Bob turned the ship over to Dan. When Bob got to the aft deck, Dave pointed to the rigging overhead. "See that turnbuckle?"

"Yes."

"What's wrong with it?"

"I don't know, maybe... say, it's got more threads showing on one end than the other!"

"Right. I'd say the end with the most threads showin' has maybe two or three threads in the barrel. If that came loose, those half-inch rods with their fittin's would carve you a new head! We got to get up there and fix that before we get into any weather. A half-inch steel rod 30 feet long weighs enough to give a man a headache, wouldn't you say?

"You bet, if he was lucky enough to survive until the things stopped dancing around the deck."

Bob stuck a crescent wrench and a pair of pliers in his pants pocket and climbed the rigging with a rope in his belt. He lashed the two ends of the stay together with a clove hitch on each end, so if it did come loose while he was securing it, it would not, hopefully, pose any danger to those on board. Additionally, all hands not involved directly with the operation were moved forward so the only concern remaining was the station wagon. That errant stay, if it became errant, could do a world of hurt to the wagon, since both the stay and the wagon were on the starboard side.

The turnbuckle was on the forward end of one of the long stays that ran from the main net outrigger to the structure at the stern, so Bob climbed up the outside of the spreader supports and hooked a leg around the outrigger. He tied the stay off, only to prevent it from swinging free if it came loose. If it separated, it was too heavy to put back together unless they were stopped in still water.

One of the boys went up the tail structure and held the rod to prevent it from turning until it had sufficiently more threads buried. They did not know for certain how many threads were in the barrel, but from the outside looking in it didn't look like there was a lot! Later, they took a turnbuckle from spares, and duplicated what was presented as rigged. There was between 1/8 and 3/16 of an inch between them and a splitting headache!

So Bob screwed the barrel onto the long end of the turnbuckle, backing it off the short end until the threads at each end were even. When he came down, he told Dave that the buckle had very few threads engaged, for it wobbled in the barrel when he first took hold of it.

The rest of the shakedown inspection was routine - a screw loose here, a bolt hanging loose in a strap there, but nothing really dangerous. All in all, they felt they now had a good boat. Jimmy was sent down to fire up the icemaker.

Joe reported as good an experience with Alpha I without the turnbuckle incident.

The boys drew straws for the schedule, going 3 hours on the wheel, 3 hours in checking systems, then 6 hours off. For this leg, Banks was the odd man out. He was available at any time, more a counselor to answer any questions from all quarters. When Rick came aboard in Puerto Rico, they went through the exercise again. Dan, as luck would have it, was the odd man out from Puerto Rico, so he was designated as cook for the trip with wheelhouse privileges. That is, he had the privilege of replacing anyone on any shift as long as it didn't interfere with his culinary responsibilities.

They had their first meal at sea, planned for weeks. Steak - those big, juicy T-bones – and were not disappointed. After that meal, they planned their menu for the whole trip, figuring steak every third dinner. That would mean they ran out of steak about the time they arrived in Africa. After that dinner, Bob felt Dan would probably have made a pretty good chef.

This schedule, of course, assumed all would go as planned, which, again, was not to be. The quiet, rhythmic *swish, swish* of the bow cutting through the water and the steady reassurance of the Caterpillar diesel were enough to lull even the most excited, uptight neophytes aboard to sound sleep. No, the only emotion that motivated any of them was anticipation. Anticipation of what tomorrow might bring.

They had passed Miami. The cities, the shores, the lights had all been left behind. Even the birds...where did the birds go? Surely they didn't fly all night...probably just plopped down on the water, on this giant waterbed. The thought made him chuckle. Bob remembered his first night on a waterbed. That was before they had designed baffles in the bed to reduce the wave action, and seasickness was a risk you took if you turned in your sleep. Funny how you never think of the little things, the many simple questions we could ask ourselves to help us understand our world better...Oh, well.

The second night was so much different from the first one. Last night they were cruising off the South Florida coast, the sky brightened by the lights of the coastal cities and Cape Canaveral, reflected from the bases of the cloud deck, the glow visible for miles. Tonight, however, there were no cities to cast their warmth, to feel akin to. There was only the occasional glimpse of the mast light of Alpha I as both boats rode the wave crests. And the throb of the engine – like a lullaby! For the most part, though, it was as if they were in different worlds. It was like a game of chance, trying to guess when the other boat would reappear. They were about a mile apart, so even when opportunity and fate confided in each other, the result was but a pinpoint of light tauntingly visible for a fleeting moment. Even if you couldn't see them, you could call on the VHF radio just to chat. That was reassuring. On *Alpha I*, either Joe or Rick would be at the helm, but he had made up his mind: Bob was not going to be the one to make the first call...unless there was an emergency or an operational question they couldn't answer. But even with Dave sacked out in the captain's cabin just a few feet away, it still got lonely. The four boys running loose helped, but the same plague affected them as well. It didn't help to have one with a bad case of loneliness try to comfort another suffering from the same ailment. Was this to be the pattern for the next month?

No, he thought, *we'd better get a handle on this before it grows out of hand. I'll talk to Joe about it when we reach San Juan. That will give us a chance to find out if it is just a passing thing or something that could be a problem.* All they had on board were some reading materials, including their Bibles. *That was it! They had talked about loneliness, complacency, and the comfort the Bible can bring. But we've got to set up regular study periods. Just like at home.*

He caught himself leaning forward, peering into the blackness off the starboard side again, and subconsciously searching for assurance that the others were still there. He shook his head, realizing he was tensing up, that he had two more hours on this watch. One of the boys would be up, probably checking the bilges, or back aft with a cup of coffee.

The throb of the engine was there, and that, too, was reassuring. He thought, *Why do I need reassurance? Why am I so up tight*? Looking ahead, he saw nothing. There was nothing out each side. His world had shrunk to the size of this wheelhouse. He even turned the spotlight on, dancing the beam across the crests. Nothing. Somewhat reconciled, his mind shifted into more pleasant thoughts, thoughts of home...sure a shame that Steve couldn't be here to enjoy this experience. Was Jo awake? Wouldn't surprise him, for many times when traveling on some overseas venture, he would awaken early only to find when returning home, that his wife was awake at the same time, wondering where he was. A wave of compassion swept over him, for he knew the bravado he exhibited at their departure was more cosmetic than genuine.

She had put up with a lot. In the early years of their marriage, it was the usual economic struggle newlyweds faced, but with them the struggle was aggravated by four boys in five years. Their daughter wasn't born until six years after that. To exist in those early years, they both worked – Bob as an engineer, Jo as a dental assistant. In 1950, engineers earned $220 a month, dental assistants somewhat less. When the opportunity arose to take on an additional load, to operate his father-in-law's dairy on a shares basis, they jumped at it. The workload was too great for Walt Mitchell, and he was faced with selling the property or getting someone to operate it on participations. Walt and Gladys Mitchell would continue to live in the big house and were eager to keep the boys, so both Bob and Jo continued in their eight to whenever jobs as well.

They built a little apartment in the old machine shed on the farm, where Jo would bake bread every Saturday. A smile crossed his face as he closed his eyes, picturing her putting six or eight loaves of fresh, homemade bread on the table. It was as if he could smell the aroma of the fresh bread and it stirred the taste sensors in him. His imagination was so captivating, so overwhelming that he felt his mouth watering. *No,* he thought, *there's nothing like fresh homemade bread.* He could still smell that inviting "come and get it" aroma. Instead, he decided to check the coffee production.

Instantly, he was shaken awake, his reverie shattered! Then he realized the radio had invaded his privacy. *Alpha I* was calling.

Joe called again, "Hello, hello *Alpha II.* Are you there?"

"Yeah, Joe, this is Bob. What's up?"

"I don't know if you're into the same stuff we're in, but if not cut about twenty degrees to starboard, towards us. We've got a phosphorescence show that beats any I've ever seen."

The captain's hatch slid open and Dave Banks climbed into the wheelhouse. "That was Joe. What's his problem?"

"No problem. He says he's into phosphorescence, and suggested we cut about twenty to starboard."

"Yeah? Well, we don't need to go chasin' him. We got our own show comin' up! Look ahead. Actually, just look down. We're in some patches of that stuff now."

"That's beautiful! What causes it?"

"I dunno. They say it's some kind of plankton. Like a firefly. Think the boys would like to see this?"

"You bet! You want to get them Dave, or should I go?"

"I'll go. I need to stretch my legs anyway."

Dan appeared in the hatch. "Hi. I was just coming up with a cup of coffee for you, when Dave said we were in some...Holy cow!! What is that?"

"That's what we're in some of. It's called phosphorescence. Dave says it's like seagoing fireflies, but they sure travel in large groups!"

Jimmy came forward, followed by Walt. By now, the *Alpha II* was plowing into the center of action and it was impossible to miss the phenomenon.

"Hey, that's so bright you could read a newspaper by it. If we had a newspaper, that is."

Jimmy was right. These spontaneous eruptions of blue-green light, some bathtub sized, and some, it appeared, the size of a whole house were so close together they gave the appearance of subterranean fluorescent lighting. It was difficult to tell how deep they were, ranging in appearance from about ten feet to thirty below the surface. They would erupt in a small area, then quickly spread like a shock wave into the surrounding sea.

Phosphorescence. Another of nature's wonders that we know little about. Webster says it's the emission of light without heat or combustion...

Dave came forward and said, "Have you told Joe what we're gonna do? He'll likely be lookin' for us to nuzzle his stern."

Almost as if on cue, the radio crackled into life again. "Alpha II, Alpha I. You guys coming over, or are you going to watch from the bleachers?»

Dave said, «Let me at him.»

«*Alpha I*, Joe, we have our own show here. Thanks for the tip. What's your heading now?"

"Okay, Dave. We're holding 140 degrees right now."

"Good. That's what we have. When do you figure we'll pick up the North Cuba light?"

"I'd say we've got time. Several hours at least, about eight, possibly nine hours depending on the visibility."

Bob figured this would be a good time to get communications set up with their home shed, so he called WOM and asked for patch through to his home.

Jo answered on the second ring. "Hello?"

"Hello, Dolly."

"Bob! Why didn't you call last night? Weren't you going to call when you got things settled? A routine established."

"Honey, I don't think there is such a thing as routine on these ships." Bob described the phosphorescence display in detail while it was still fresh in his mind. but he omitted the turnbuckle incident. She was pretty uptight about the majority of her family sailing off into the sunrise, perhaps never to be seen again! Prior to their departure, they had had a number of discussions along this line, all of which left him a little down, but the anticipation of the adventure and of the boys' exuberance always revived him. Their position was now just abeam of Grand Bahama and even as they passed, a Norwegian Cruise Line ship the *Skyward* set out from Port Everglades, a testimony of reality. It, too, was headed through the islands, but was about a mile behind them, and off their starboard stern. As soon as she was clear of the close in private boat traffic, she set out for her destination, wherever that was – San Juan and points east. The Norwegian ships were capable of about 35 knots, and compared with their 91/2 or 10 knots, the Alphas reminded Bob of a drag racer whose engine failed at the starting gate. On open water you only have about 13 miles visibility at eye level height because of the curvature of the earth.

In less than 30 minutes of passing them, she was "hull down" - out of sight.

Yes, this could be long voyage!

After their amazement at the speed at which the *Skyward* disappeared, with her lights all ablaze, they continued their conversation to develop a schedule where they could call when the girlfriends and wives could be present to relate the goings-on in each little world. Of course, Rick was aboard the *Alpha I,* and was not a party to this arrangement until later when he joined them on the *Alpha II.* However, he did make similar contacts through the ship-to-shore patch to his home in Largo, Florida. He and Bobi (nee Roberta) had been married less than a year. Dan and Debi had just been married in mid-May, and in a way this could be considered Dan's one-person honeymoon. It's a shame he did not have his bride along. Walt was "going steady" with Cindy (whom he married as soon as this trip was over and Walt returned from Ghana! – mute testimony of the truth in the old adage, "Absence makes the heart grow fonder.")

Bob and Dave Banks divided up the duties for the night ahead, with Dan and Dave on the wheel until midnight, then Bob and Walt would have it until six A.M. Then Jimmy, under Dave Banks' direction, would get the day started. That should bring them about as close to Cuba as they would want to come.

Two were assigned on each watch. One, of course, was on the helm and the other had a list of duties ranging from housekeeping to operational, to safety items that he was responsible for, in order to turn the boat over to the next crew in a seaworthy condition. All in all, both Alpha boats came through their **[second]** day clean, except for the turnbuckle.

Bob was lost in deep sleep in the Captain's cabin when he was rudely awakened by a commotion in the wheelhouse. "What do you mean there's no power to the stove?"

"That's all! There's no electrical power to the stove!

By the time Bob got topside, Banks had already checked the electrical load center on the aft bulkhead of the wheelhouse. "Yep, they's no AC power. Dan, run below and see if the Kohler is runnin'. If not, that may be our problem. If it is, then we got a problem in the electrical generatin' or distributin' circuits! Either way, we got to get hold of Desco, and get them working on it!" To no one in particular,

Dave asked, "What time is it?" "Six-fifteen, a little after six, and quarter after six. "Three responses, take your pick."

But Dave reached overhead for the VHF. "*Alpha II. Alpha I*, come back".

"Yeah, Dave, What's up?"

"Joe, we don't know yet, but our AC power just fell off the line. That means we don't have the icemaker, no cook stove, no refrigerator, and no air conditioning. But we still have radios. Just wanted to give you heads up over here."

"Thanks. Have you tried Desco yet?" Joe asked.

"No, they're next. Oh, Bob's got them on the fifteen meter band now. Guess I'd better go. We'll keep you up to date."

Desco's lead mechanic and spares supervisor were both on the line. Dave Banks took the mike from Bob, and said, "Hello, who's this?"

"This is Ron Allbright. I'm the lead mechanic today, for this shift anyway. You boys got a problem?"

Dave acknowledged, "If a hundred pounds of T-bone steaks headed on a spoil course, without the ability to brew the likeness of a cup of coffee to wash it down wasn't a problem, then I'm not sure what would be!"

Ron gave them several more things to check to get a better handle on the problem. When he was finished Banks stood up and announced to all present, "Well Gents, we got our hands full. Who wants to help track this critter down?" With one accord, every one of the boys volunteered for duty. So Dave got his charges together and headed them toward the after hatch. "Walt, I understand you are to be the mechanic on this boat out of San Juan."

"Yessir, so I understand."

'Well, I don't think there's going to be room for all of us down beside the Kohler to run what Ron wanted, so Jimmy, why don't you bring a pad and a pencil, you can take notes. And Walt, you and I can check her out, OK? The rest of you can stay up topside, but first, see how many empty Coke cans you can scrounge up.

Empty them and rinse them out, then fill them three quarters full of the drinking water, such as it is, that we have on board. Then, we're going to put them up there on the exhaust manifold of the Cat. But be careful, that manifold is hot, hot, hot. Should make pretty good coffee, though. May even get us into San Juan where we can trade this load of crappy antifreeze off for some real decent coffee makin' material."

But Bob was troubled. Signs of lethargy were still there, elevated a little by the current problems, or was that just his imagination? He figured he and Joe Shell must split for a dinner together when they reach San Juan to talk about that problem, and what might be done about it. Tedium. The most insidious, unwanted extra baggage on a long voyage, or long flight, particularly over water at night. And the longest, and thus the most tedious part of the voyage was fast approaching. It was a problem common to both men. Bob, from the standpoint that he would have a group of well behaved, but still volatile young men to ride herd on, and Joe, with a crew of native hands many of whom had not been aboard a vessel as large as this, despite their many years collectively as crewmen on the small craft that plied the coastal waters off Ghana. Or the two that had crew experience aboard the larger coastal steamers despite the reports Joe had received of their previous experience. Their compatibility, their desire to work together would have to be determined by their performance. One question remained. These men had been chosen by the government. Neither Joe Shell, Dave Banks, nor Bob had any idea what criteria was used in the selection process. For all they knew, selection may have come down to who was the cousin or nephew of whom. That was not a far stretch of imagination. Mutiny had been triggered by far less than the elements that could be seen lurking here. Over the next day and a half, they would have to find time to explore this envisioned problem. And out of San Juan, Dave would be part of the two-man police force to keep peace, harmony and productivity in place aboard *Alpha I*, and to fashion the Ghanaians into reasonable likenesses of trawler seamen.. On the *Alpha II*, there was only an occasional indication of perceived resistance on Walt's part to pull his share of the load. Walt was the youngest, and with three older brothers, he held a bit of an inferiority complex, one reason Bob made him engineer/maintenance man this trip – the other was Walt's ability to devise solutions to baffling problems. Walt was more than smart. Bob's boys were always free thinkers, starting at the top with Steve and working downward to Walt. Jimmy fit right in the line, somewhere between Dan and Walt. Walt's was an inventive mind, one that was fed by challenges.

So far, they had enjoyed fair skies, to the end that most days two (and occasionally all three) boys could be found on top of the wheelhouse, both a sunbathing site and a lookout tower. But the breeze was freshening. Dave noted, "Could be that some weather is movin' in."

"Porpoises!" One of them exclaimed. There were six or seven of them running with the boat, keeping about ten to twenty yards to starboard.

Dave's comment passed by unnoticed.

Bob queried Dave, saying, "Dave, what did you just say?

"I said 'it looks like we got some weather movin' in." Dave called the boys and said, "Boys, I don't want to throw water on your on your fun time, but I think the job that needs to be done now is to dress the deck down. Get all loose items stowed and the ship rigged for a blow!"

The prow was cleared in an instant, and those who were involved were stringing lifelines. One by one they drifted back to the bow, gathered on the prow peering into the water, where the protective group of porpoises had reassembled, in flawless precision formation like P-51 escorts on a raid into Germany during WWII. Every so often, one or two would split off and give boys a show - jumps, rolls, then take up their positions again at the bow.

Bob wondered, *How could I have been so stupid to have believed lethargy was growing to monumental proportions? I will have that little discussion with Banks, and dinner with Joe. Just look at those boys! They are totally absorbed in what they are witnessing and doing. Charley was right. If the rest of this voyage is as interesting as these first few days have been, this will be an experience they will never forget. They got the deck cleared and secured in record time.*

Then the boys went back to watching the porpoises.
Not long after the porpoises finished their clowning around for those aboard *Alpha II*, Jimmy said, "We've got a boat coming up on our right side."

Dave Banks jumped right in, "Jimmy! That's, there's a vessel comin' up on our starboard side. Got it?"

"Yessir, Capt. Dave, 'Vessel, starboard'. Got it".

All hands were watching the oncoming tug. Dave said, "That's the "Borinquen." I used to know one of her Captains. That boat totes 1800 horsepower under the hood. Look how much water she's pushing with no load. She's going to rock us pretty good after she passes." She gave a couple of short blasts on the horn, so Dave answered with a couple of his own. "Believe she's going to San Juan as well, but she will certainly beat us there. The Borinquen had six men working on the aft deck. They all stopped to watch the *Alpha II* slide off aft.

"Did you ever wonder how they got the name 'tug' boats? Well, I'll tell you. When the longer range coastal vessels reached their destinations, they proved to be too bulky and did not have the maneuverability necessary to make way in harbor traffic, so the answer was found in wooden rowboats that would turn these clipper ships and others, line them up with docking space, and nuzzle them into dock. But keep in mind, many of these early transports were wind powered, which complicated maneuvering in the harbors. They were called 'tug' boats simply because their 'harbor power' was provided by the oarsmen tugging at the oars. Some of these 'tug' boats had sixteen oarsmen. Then, in the 1800s, I think about 1830, a steam-powered tug boat appeared and revolutionized the river traffic and the harboring industry. The equipment has grown to keep pace with the enormous strides the shipping industry has made. That one that just passed us was only ten feet longer than this boat, but she has 1800 horsepower! Compare that to our 360 horsepower, but, then, we're not pushing Queen Mary-sized vessels around, are we?"

"Dan, did you ever crew on one of those tugs?" Walt asked.

"Yep, I was about you boys' age, when I figured the sea was large enough to keep me occupied for one lifetime, so I had the chance at a job and took it. On one of them tugs, you work. It ain't no bed of roses. Well, if it is, I'll tell you, they forgot to strip the thorns off of the bed they gave me! Oh, you get lots of time to goof off, just like the crew on the Borinquen was doin', but when you get into movin' ships in the harbor, there's little time for relaxation. You see, housekeeping becomes all important. You got to keep all unused lines coiled, so they are ready for use yet out of the way so no one trips over them when the crew gets busy. It's a long road to command one of those tugs, and that's what I wanted to do. Not necessarily a tug, you understand, but command a ship. With tugs, it's a long, hard road, so I kinda backed into fishin'. Crew turnover is far greater, so if a person has the desire and the moxie, opportunity comes up much faster."

That night off the coast of Cuba, Dave's observations of the weather were realized. Dave suggested the deck be re-checked and all loose items be cleared while they still had a little twilight to work with. He got Joe on the VHF, and found Joe was one step ahead. His deck was secured already, except for one thing which they were to learn about within a few hours.

It hit them about midnight, and Dave called it the Granddaddy of all squall lines. In short order, it was creating twelve-to-fourteen-foot mountains of black waves washing over both boats, rocking the boats mercilessly and turning the Ghanaians forty shades of green.

The motion in the *Alpha I* was so violent that no one could stand up or head to the rail, if they wanted to, and all of the Ghanaians did need the rail but given their situation, they just rolled to the side of their bunks and let go.

Aboard the *Alpha I*, Joe and Rick shared the same bunk, for it didn't take long to realize the native crew were not outfitted with sea legs. In addition, the crews' quarters on both Alpha boats only had four bunks. Both Joe and Rick said they would not stay in the crew cabin. As soon as the ship began bucking and twisting with the effects of the winds and twelve-foot seas, it made venturing outside the cabin dangerous, but it also created the additional problem. The Ghanaian crew was seasick! It started with one crewman then because of the close quarters it rapidly spread to the rest of the crew, except for Joe and Rick. It was Rick's turn at the wheel, Joe having sacked out. There was a repeated loud thump, as if something heavy was rolling around, in the bow area. Rick was alarmed so he woke Joe Shell, who staggered to life. Thump!...Thump, Thump!

Joe dashed to the searchlight control and flicked it on. After the next couple of waves struck the *Alpha I*, Joe saw the problem. He announced, "They didn't tie our anchor down and it's sliding around on the foredeck." He cocked his head and said, "One of us is going to have to go out and tie that sucker down, or we'll have no wheelhouse by morning." The cocked head and the imploring eyes told Rick he was to be the sacrificial lamb for this journey. "Here, Rick, I'll tie this line around your waist just in case you run into any trouble."

"What kind of trouble might I run into?"

Joe just rolled his eyes in the general direction of the wind and seas outside.

Rick said, "How much does that anchor weigh?"

"You know, Rick, I've never had scales with me when handling them, but one man can usually lift one, so I imagine they would weigh in at about forty, maybe fifty pounds."

"OK, enough said." Rick was going through mental gymnastics regarding the best way to subdue the anchor, given the fact that it apparently had a mind of its own. The more he thought about it, the more apprehensive he became. Color was draining from his face – *that* he could feel. His normally ruddy complexion was slowly being replaced by that pasty, pale gray color commonly associated with death or dying! At the same time, he became increasingly conscious of beads of sweat breaking out along his upper lip, and a cold, clammy feeling as sweat permeated his upper torso. His legs were made of sponge rubber. He felt the sweat now running freely down his back as he contemplated the challenge in front of him. He took two deep breathes, waited for a wave to clear the foredeck, and stepped through the port hatch. The wind took his breath away. It was far more vicious than it looked from inside the wheelhouse. Rick ducked back around the corner against the wheelhouse to get his bearings and to re-plan his attack on the anchor in light of the wind.

The wind had not slackened. Rick timed the waves, noting they were coming aboard every seven to ten seconds. Every third wave seemed to offer a bit more time between it and the succeeding one and the anchor was being washed from the wheelhouse to the prow area and back with devastating regularity with almost every wave. Equally menacing were the mountainous waves.

The free end of the lifeline was made fast on the underpinnings of the captain's chair, and Rick determined the line tied about him had been secured as well. He waited until the shifting anchor settled down between waves, figuring he had about ten seconds before the next wave would strike. Rick and Joe had discussed the securing of the anchor to hold it in place until they got into calmer seas, if there were calmer seas in their future. So Rick waited at the leeward side of the wheelhouse hatch until the anchor slid to a stop, then dashed out around the corner of the wheelhouse and dove on the anchor. The wind hit him full in the face and took his breath away. He looped a couple of turns around the anchor shaft and tied it off before the next wave hit, sending the anchor and Rick forward against the cleat, Rick thought, *That's an ideal place to tie this off*. He looped two turns around the cleat and the next wave hit the boat. She shook, but the anchor stayed put. Rick was washed back against the wheelhouse, and then crawled back to the anchor to finish the job. He used the rest of the line to loop around the cleat using a seaman's reverse loop to secure it, then he tied the loose end off on the anchor. Before he finished, one of those watery mountains came crashing down on him, sending him right back against the wheelhouse. A very wet Rick just rested against the wheelhouse and when the next wave cleared, staggered to his feet and made it inside.

Joe exclaimed, "That was a magnificent job! We may be able to make a sailor out of you yet!" Rick thought, *The only thing I need right now, is to dry off and get some dry clothes on, but if that's what it takes to be a sailor, I'm happy just where I am.*

Meanwhile, on Alpha II, the noose of concern was growing ever tighter with each crashing wave. Each mountain of evidence of the seas dominant authority gave indication that this wave may be the one that flips them over, and they meet their maker in some watery habitat far from family, far from home. These thoughts raced wildly through their minds. Each thought leaving an indelible scar on their confidence. The boat was being battered from starboard and astern In between these morbid thoughts was one of concern for Alpha I. They had no concept of the battle facing he Alpha II's crew. But Alpha I had its own problem. Rick was faced with that 50 pound wrecking ball wreaking havoc on the control center, the wheelhouse of Alpha I.

Every so often, a new, ominous noise would come forth from within the Alpha II, now a gratng, then a spine tingling screech reminiscent of grade school days when the teacher would purposefully, they believed, create the same sound with a piece of chalk on the blackboard, in fiendish glee just to keep the students of that day awake. Today, it had the same effect . To this cacophony of sound was added a loud sporadic banging, eventually traced to cooking utensils being dislodged, and bouncing around the galley. They gave an excellent impression of a steel drum band in some rag time rendition of "Mairzey Doats".

The next day, sailing along the north coast of Hispanola, the weather began to clear. The azure blue sky gave no hint of any inclement weather.

SLEEP, IT'S WHERE YOU CAN FIND IT! : **Dan Murray**, caught a few zzzzzz's.

The pots and pans stayed stowed and all could get a lttle much needed shut-eye. Bob mused this must be a trying place for a weatherman to earn his keep. Mistakes in forecasts are to be expected. Then he remembered this was just the beginning of the hurricane season, and they would be headed right up the barrel of the Northern Hemisphere's major weather maker. But the sight of land, palm trees, beaches, and villages erased any trepidation that lingered. It had been three days since they had seen land, any land. They had purposefully run well north of Cuba, having no desire to get into an argument with a Cuban gunboat. Besides, Bob didn't speak Spanish, and neither did Dave. As for Joe, he wasn't sure. It just made more sense to stay clear. No need to tempt fate.

AFTER STORM NO. 1 : **Cap'n Bob** doing his share. Note the uniform of the trip. The ouriggs still down.

The VHF crackled to life. "Dave, Bob, either of you guys awake?"

Bob answered, "What do you mean, after a night like last night,we're all awake. What's up?"

"Bob, I'm glad it's you, 'cause I know Dave has been here before, and we've got several more hours before we reach the San Juan breakwater. It is constructed of rocks that extend out about two, maybe three miles, so don't get fixed on looking for the entrance buoy or the San Juan lighthouse. You'll see the light before you get lined up with the entrance to the harbor. If you head for it too soon, you may end up docking on a rock pile. I've got an eye on you, so I'm coming over. You want to stay about four miles off until you pick up the light."

STILL STORM NO. 1 : Stack coated with salt.

"Tell you what Joe, you come on over and we'll stay in your shadow until we're in the harbor."

"OK."

"Dan, who all is up back there?"

"We're all awake, if that's what you mean."

"Good, round up the troops and come up front."

When the boys were assembled in the wheelhouse, Bob addressed them, "You remember when the Kohler fell off line, what, two nights ago? Well, we're going to be in port soon, and I suppose there is some stuff in the hold that won't pass the smell test and it stands to reason we should get rid of it out here, particularly those five dozen eggs we started out with, and the steaks. Dan, take a small pan below and check a few of those eggs. If they are beginning to smell like rotten eggs, get rid of them."

"OK. Jimmy, why don't you come too, just in case my smeller is busted?"

They sampled four or five eggs. The first two were passable, the third was not, and the fourth was putrid. So they determined that, given the time in port until the Kohler was fixed, all the eggs would probably have gone the way of those before. So they proceeded to chuck them up through the hatch and over the side. It looked like good entertainment to Walt, so he invited himself to the party. Then, someone got the bright idea that they should have a target to throw at. It did not seem to make any difference in their marksmanship. The fact that they were pitching the eggs from the forward port corner of the hold through the hatch amidships about twenty feet aft of their pitcher's mound. So it was quite a test of the boys' ability to get an egg through that maze and over the side without corrupting the ship. When Dave saw what was happening - broken eggs on the starboard rails, in the hold, and on the deck – he called Bob and asked him if he was guilty of authorizing this mayhem.

Bob admitted that he did tell them to get rid of those eggs if they were going bad, but not to plaster half-rotten eggs over their home for the next month. He had them get the water hose out and wash the aft deck down with sea water. They also did a cursory job on the few eggs that had not made it out of the hold – the latter done with soap, water, and brushes.

chapter nine

SAN JUAN, PUERTO RICO

It was more than six hours later. They were passing by El Morrow, a fortification that figured prominently in the Spanish American war and into the harbor of Old San Juan. The harbor was actually two harbors, split in the center by a service island, with two ocean-going cargo vessels tied up. One of these vessels was the *Mayaguez*, of North Korean fame. She had just returned from the impounding by North Korea and was moored on the west side of the service island, undergoing repair after the impounding.

As they approached the island, all on board became fascinated with the scenery around Dorado. In the background they could see the hills behind San Juan, which elated all of them. All but Dave. He was surveying the area of the Dorado Hotel, a resort hotel with a well-populated beach, a local haven for mermaids.

Joe was on VHF channel 16, and got someone in the harbormaster's office. They directed the boats down the east side of the harbor. Joe spoke, "I see where we're going, I think! There's about 200 feet of dock space open ahead on the port side." On *Alpha II*, the boys got the lines ready. Joe and Rick had their native crew busy with the same tasks, and the *Alpha I* slid into position against the bumpers made from old tires, and fastened to the dock. It was a concrete dock, built for vessels of the Alpha boat's size, which made access to and from the boats very handy.

The boys tied off the *II*, and coiled the excess lines. Bob shut the engine down. And it was silent. No one realized how much a part of their living that Cat had taken over. The silence was deafening. But when Bob cleaned up the wheelhouse, he looked up [a-]right into the face of a uniformed officer.

"Good evening, Sir. Where are you coming from?"

"St. Augustine, Florida, bound for Tema, Ghana."

"You will be moving out, then?"

"Well, we do have a problem, and parts were shipped by Eastern Airlines, but yes, then we will be moving on." Joe Shell walked up. The officer said, "Do you have your ship's papers?"

"Yes, Sir."

"Bring them with you, and come inside to the office." It was spoken as an invitation, not as an order. Bob asked, "Do you want to see papers on both boats?"

"That would be fine." So Bob and Joe got their papers and followed the officer inside. They were overwhelmed at what they saw in there. There was every conceivable type of workout equipment imaginable. The officer explained, "This is the training facility for the San Juan Police Department. During the day it is pretty busy, but as you can see, at night there's really not much going on. If you boys want to work out a bit, we'd love to have you."

Joe and Bob outlined the purpose of the trip, and the fact that they had four Ghanaian crewmembers aboard the *Alpha I.* These four did have their passports and were on the crew member manifest, but the officer citing regulations wished to see them with their passports. Joe had them in short order. Concern was written all over their faces in any language! But the officer, whose name was Felix, set them at ease. They were not in any trouble, and they weren't being deported – everything was A-OK! But they could not be released to wander around San Juan unless their Captain assumed responsibility for them. They understood, for the protocol had been thoroughly described to them before they got on board in St. Augustine. Now a portion of their visible happiness returned. They could return to the cleanup undertaken when they ran into the squall line.

All was in order, so Bob thanked Felix, and said, "We promised the boys a real meal as soon as we landed, so I think it's a good time to honor our word."

But Joe piped in, "Bob, with all you and the boys have gone through the last few days, I rather imagine a decent meal is pretty near the top of your want list. But,

I've got to excuse myself. I have friends here I called before we left and told them I would call when we reached port. So, please just count me out for tonight. Dave is familiar with Old San Juan. I'm sure he can point you to a reasonably good restaurant."

They stepped outside to face all four boys and Dave Banks, all who were waiting with hands and faces washed and their hair combed. "Going somewhere?" Bob queried. "Whose black book did you lift?"

Then Felix renewed his invitation to work out in their training facility. "I'll have to clear it with my superiors but we've done it before so, I don't think it will be any problem. And about the aliens aboard your boat, I'll be here until at least midnight so go get a decent meal. Just go out to the main road, turn right and keep walking."

When they reached the main road, they felt the six days at sea. Walt said, "This sidewalk doesn't want to stay still."

Walt wasn't alone. The seven of them looked like a bunch of drunken sailors. They were all staggering Add to that the giddiness of their newfound freedom. The scene was reminiscent of VJ day when the joy of the world boiled over, and was so infectious that everyone was caught up in it. The restaurant they were led to by Dave was an apparently popular after-theatre meeting spot. Walt complained again about the room going around. Menus were passed round, and the waitress asked for their drink orders. All ordered coffee except Dave Banks, who ordered black coffee and a beer! Maybe it was a beer and black coffee! Bob asked how their steaks were, and the waitress answered, "Well everything is good here, but we serve a lot of them, particularly the rib eye."

Bob responded, "Sold! Medium rare." The boys all picked steaks as well, since all but Rick had been deprived of steak for three…no, four days. When it was served, they dug in like there was no tomorrow. Walt mentioned again that he wished the room would stay still, that it would realize that they were back on dry land again!

Dave said, "Rick, we'll swap ships in the morning, if that's all right with you."

"That's fine. I learned a lot from Joe, but it will be nice to get our group together again."

Bob said, "Fine, but keep in mind we've a lot to do before we can shove off here."

"Like what?" One of the boys asked.
"Like, I've got to pick up our parts from Eastern, and I don't know about the rest of you, but I would like to have a couple of you work on reasonable menus for this last leg, then we have to go shopping. You guys remember the steaks we had on board about a week ago? I'd like to think we're going to replace them with something more edible. And that hold stinks and it's going to get cleaned before we pull away from this dock. Now, I've a little surprise for you. You know that officer Joe and I were talking to? That was Felix. He's from the San Juan Police Department, Marine Division, and the place where we tied up is their dock. They say we are welcome to stay right there until we get the *II* fixed. Now for the good part. That building they are in is their training facility! And we can use it. It's got about any conceivable workout machine you can imagine, and they have showers in there. The Ghanaians can use it as well, as long as a responsible member of our crew is with them. Otherwise, they're pretty well confined to the ship."

The waitress asked for dessert orders, and Walt was the first of the pack. "Yes, I'd take a chocolate sundae." With no sweets for a week the thought of ice cream or pie, or both, was too tempting for their weakened taste buds to resist. As she left the table, a well-dressed couple was being seated at the table to their right. The desserts came, and they had not lost all their appetites on rib eyes.

Walt's stomach picked that time to register its unease. Walt picked up the bread-basket, removed the remaining bread, and upchucked his entire dinner into the bread basket! He then asked the waiteress to "Please get rid of this."

The couple at the next table took this all in, looked at each other then slowly rose, folded their menus and exited the restaurant! Bob ushered the boys out the door and paid the bill while the waitress surveyed Walt's latest contribution to San Juan dining.

Back at the dock Dan, Bob, and several of the boys visited with Felix, with the thought of getting a shower. Felix showed them where the fresh towels were, and where the used ones should be put, then wished them a good evening.

The showers aboard were sufficient, but were, for the most part, the seawater variety which left you feeling like you were not finished, that you had not yet showered. A bucket of lazarette rinse water did much to alleviate that feeling, but was at best, an ersatz substitute for a wholesome cleansing.

The next day dawned as usual, severe clear and visibility unlimited, and the crew made the most of it. The first order of business was to clean the hold. Walt, Dan and Jimmy went into the hold to rid the Alpha II of any reminders of their difficulties with the AC power. The T-bone steaks were well received by the host of not wild, but homeless canines roaming the banks of the harbor. Overnight, the *Alpha II* became a sort of "doggie deli" to them.

Joe and Rick cast off for the Texaco docks on the opposite shore of the harbor to top the fuel onboard in *Alpha I*. Bob made arrangements with Eastern Airlines to pick up the parts shipped down by Desco. Since there were no charges on the shipment, arrangements were made to allow a representative from San Juan Diesel Service to pick up the parts. The mechanic from SJDS, along with a helper and a prodigious amount of tools, arrived at Alpha II. Prior to their arrival, Bob's feeling was that Walt should hang next to the mechanic to learn all he could about the Kohler and what could go wrong with it. Normally the Kohler was a very simple, trouble-free unit, but they reasoned that they would be another two weeks or more on the open sea. Bob, Joe, and Cap'n Dave felt it would make more sense to have as much know-how aboard regarding the normally trouble free Kohler, given their experiences so far on this voyage. Each ship carried 500 feet of one-inch tow line, in the event a tow was necessary plus the cable spooled upon the winches. So they were not as much concerned about being dead in the water as they were about to be without cooking or refrigeration capabilities. Three days without either proved to be enough for them all.

When Joe and Rick got to Texaco they found that Texaco Accra had done exactly as they said. Texaco San Juan had been on alert for over a day, and knew about *Alpha II's* Kohler problems from Desco. Joe only had 9000 gallons of fuel aboard *Alpha I* to start this voyage, and normally that would probably have been sufficient, given calm winds and favorable seas, but Joe figured if he was going to err, it was going to be on the conservative side. That philosophy had served them wee in the past in the past, and he saw no reason to change now. *Alpha II* had about 11,200 gallons aboard when it departed from St. Augustine. Both boats had burned a little over 1000 gallons apiece in the six days to San Juan – around 200 gallons per day, or looking at it another way, 9,000 gallons would take them out for 45 days. All three men concluded that if they hadn't found Africa by then, they had more severe problems to contend with. Nine thousand gallons was considered sufficient to get there and spend two or three days searching the area and dragging for fish before coming to port.

As *Alpha I* rounded the island where the Mayaguez was docked, Joe spotted several workboat types standing off the fuel docks, and said to Rick, " I should have called Texaco on the VHF to see how stacked up they were for fuel. It looks like they have a line formed up over there."

"Where?"

"See the tank farm, where all those big tanks are? Do you see the one that says 'Texaco'?"

"Yes."

"Well, just in front of that, and a little to the right do you see a few workboat types just sitting, waiting?"

"I see some boats, but I can't tell if they are workboats or not."

"Here, take the glasses," he said, handing the binoculars to Rick.

Meanwhile Joe was on the VHF, "*Alpha I* to Texaco San Juan."

"*Alpha I*, Texaco, five square. What can I do for you?"

"Just wondering what your backlog looked like now for no.1 or no. 2 diesel. We need about 1000 gallons."

"Bring it on in, we can have you loaded and underway in forty-five minutes or so."

"Sounds good. We are mid-channel heading your way."

"Rick, you heard that?"

"Yes, and I gather it didn't make much difference that you didn't call them before heading over here."

"Yes, but common courtesy suggests that you contact them to get a place in the queue. This will work out fine. Your dad and I have dinner planned tonight to go over ships' stores for the rest of the voyage. I know he asked those who were with him the first leg to make a realistic list of foods they would like to see on board for the rest of the journey, but I didn't know if he got to you."

"Yes, he let me know, and I'm going to go over it with him tomorrow morning."

So far, the Ghanaians were content to have access to the galley and had designated one of their own as chief cook and bottle washer. While in port, they were introduced to a staple of the Puerto Ricans (compliments of the police cook), rice and red beans. They later learned rice and black beans was a Cuban staple food, and Joe opted to stock a few packages of black beans to compliment the red ones for a little variety. Besides, Joe preferred rice and black beans, which was also a staple of the Dominican Republic.

The fuelling completed, they secured the deck, and headed back across the harbor. When they tied up, they found that Dan and Jimmy had scrubbed the hold so that it was almost habitable. Walt worked with the San Juan diesel services mechanic most of the afternoon, and learned a lot about the Kohler. Bob was in his cabin, having showered, courtesy of the police, and was now cleaning up for a seven o'clock dinner with Joe. As the boys finished their assignments for the day, they went to the gym for some hoops and a workout, and best of all, a shower. Dave Banks was responsible for cleaning up the drinking water. He ran two full tanks through the onboard plumbing with marked success, but not what one could call a complete victory. The water retained a slight reminder of what used to be, but as Dave Banks had said, "It ain't gonna kill you." The boys increased the number of soft drinks to be brought aboard to three cases.

Banks had offered to stay on board with the Ghanaians and the boys decided they would find a hamburger for Dave somewhere as long as it was not near their stop the previous night!

At seven, Joe called from the dock, "Bob, you ready?"

"You bet. You know San Juan, where would you like to go?"

"I was thinking about that. There's a good restaurant in connection with a marina up at the end of the harbor overlooking the harbor activities called 'Club Nautico'. Is that OK?"

"Sounds good to me. Do they have good food?"

"It's the best seafood I've found in San Juan!. Do you like seafood?"

"I love it if it is fresh."

"You would have to swim with the fishes to get it any fresher."

"Rick, Dan, we're leaving."

As they walked, Joe said, "Bob, you were right in wanting to bring things on board to keep the boys occupied. It's going to get next door to boredom on the way across. There won't be any porpoises trying to outrun us, or any phosphorescence to light our night. And we would hope there will be stars in all their glory, since some of the boys are stargazers, but it's a very poor **time to find out** if you've depended on that, that you were wrong. At times we'll be over 1000 miles from the nearest land, unless you measure it straight down."

Joe continued, "I'd ask them what games they like to play, and get two or three on board to help relieve the boredom that's bound to set in."

When Bob and Joe finally made it to the Club Nautico, dinner guests were arriving, but the Maitre'd seated them at a table in front of one of five floor-to-ceiling windows that graced the east wall overlooking the ever prominent Mayaguez. Dusk was just falling and Bob had started to make note of things discussed on the walk there. The combination of failing light outside, and the subdued light inside, made note-taking impractical. Both men had little choice but to study the menu in the faint light.

The room erupted in a flash of light and noise like cannon fire filled its confines, followed closely by red, green, and yellow eruptions. This display obscured any detail left inside the restaurant and all attention was directed outside. The Mayaguez picked up every hue of the myriad of colors subjected to it.

Bob exclaimed, "What is going on?" Then, and only then, did it dawn on him. This was the Fourth of July, a national holiday in The United States. Even though Puerto Rico was a commonwealth [] under protection by the U.S., the extravaganza witnessed by these men belied the fact that this was supposed to be a U.S. celebration. It obviously was not confined to the U.S.

Bob said, "I wonder if the boys are taking this in?"

Joe countered with, "I wouldn't worry about the boys, I was thinking about Dave and the Ghanaians! The boys know about July Fourth. The Ghanaians, I don't think, have a clue as to how we behave this time of the year, and heaven only knows there's been enough whistles, screaming and bangs here to wake the dead! I only hope we'll find them all when we get back."

"You're right. For someone in a strange land, that would be a wild, wild wake up party! Particularly if you're not expecting it."

At Joe's suggestion, both had ordered a lobster dish, Joe a conventional steamed lobster, and Bob a combination "turf and surf." "Delicioso!" declared Joe, apparently his limit in Spanish, and Bob confirmed their satisfaction with the meal. Over coffee, a rich dark roast Puerto Rican blend, they got busy with the largest single item on the list of stores necessary to ease the crossing. They added long-life milk, several boxes of Cheerios, and prodigious amounts of beef jerky along with the three cases of Pepsi, some extra rice, a few steaks for variety, and the five pounds of bacon Bob thought of earlier. The bacon would keep well and would augment the five pounds of Crisco they put on board in St. Augustine.

Joe had been successful in his search for powdered eggs and long-life milk – milk processed so that as long as it remains unopened, it will stay fresh for an extended period. The crew transfer between Rick and Dave was underway and as time permitted, final workouts were also added to the final preparations, followed by a shower in the police compound.

Bob, Joe and Dave Banks were aboard the *II* having coffee when Felix came aboard. He said, "Men, I just wanted to tell you that you and your boys are welcome to come back here any time. And frankly, the more I see of you, the more excited I am for you. In fact, I wish I was going with you. So, you plan to be out today?"

Joe answered him, "Yes, it looks like three or four this afternoon we should be all ready to roll on. And we would all be amiss if we didn't tell you how much we appreciate your hospitality, and the ability to get our equipment repaired, and the showers. Yes, especially the showers."

Dave interjected, "You bet, 'cause we was getting pretty ripe after only six days out. We got another couple of weeks or so yet."

"The pleasure, I assure you, was all ours. All of you have been perfect gentlemen. It's been a real pleasure to know you. And your alien crew, they have been remarkable. Never a harsh word. I'm certain you will have good trip."

Bob said, "Thank you, Felix. Felix, we appreciate your comments, but there was one thing you said that warrants a revision to our sailaway checklist which we're working on now."

Dave questioned, "What's that?"

"Based on one of Felix's last comments, we'd better add a search of all hidden corners on these rigs just to make sure our papers are still in order when we get to the other side. Stowaways are not on our manifest!"

After a little more good-natured verbal sparring and a tour of the *II*, Felix went back inside, and the three men got back to working in Bob's cabin where Joe had spread a chart of the east coast of Puerto Rico and the U.S.Virgin Islands on the chart table. A line had been drawn from San Juan around Fajardo on the northeast coast of Puerto Rico south of the islands of Culebra and north of Vieques, both parts of Puerto Rico, then to the east past St. Thomas, St. John, and Tortolla. Joe said, "If we're going to leave today, I thought we should have an idea as to where we're going. Better to do it here than discuss it over the VHF, don't you think?"

"When we leave out of San Juan, we're going to be on the south edge of the San Juan deep with no real problems as far as rock outcroppings are concerned, but when we turn the corner at Fajardo, we begin to run along the shelf that spawns about fifty or sixty small islands that make up the U.S.Virgins. That can be a little tricky. It's been a couple of years since I've been through there, but it's pretty clear what we learned then. So I'd suggest we go single file through this area. That's about the last hazardous area we should see for the remainder of the trip."

"You mean, all the way to Africa?"

"Yes, Bob, except if we run into weather. Past Barbuda it is a straight run across the ocean."

"Well, what is the possibility of running into weather?"

"Your guess is as good as mine."

"When we're flying, we have weather reports generated constantly forecasting adverse weather so we can adjust our plans. Isn't there a marine weather reporting system? I'm sure there is, otherwise how could they forecast hurricanes and tropical depressions?"

"OK, you got me. There are a number of marine weather broadcasts on various frequencies which you'll find in the Coastal Pilot along with the time they broadcast weather."

"Let's make a final check of our stores, make sure we've received all we have ordered, and we know where it is. When we pull out of here there is no 7/11s between here and Africa, right?"

"That's for certain," said Dave. "Bob, I don't remember seeing a refer truck to bring your perishables. Did anyone reschedule them? As I remember, they were scheduled to be here tomorrow just before our sail away."

Joe added, "I made the original order for delivery, and I haven't changed it. Let me go inside that and call them, see what we can work out."

Joe went into the office to use the telephone, and found the supplier had a truck scheduled for *Alpha II* the next morning, that they did not have anything for today since they had three cruise ships in port, the first departing early the next morning. The best they could do was to adhere to the original schedule.

When Joe returned and broke the news, he also had a suggestion. "It looks like we're stuck here for another day, unless you're willing to forego any fresh meats and fruits, and some other stuff, Bob. Let's go back to the original schedule. Dave, you've always spoken of El Morrow as if it held some special fascination for you. Why don't you take the boys on a tour of the fort? You could do that today or in the morning."

"Hey, count me in. I've never seen that either," Bob interjected. "How long would that tour take us?"

Dan said, "It can take as little as four hours, or all day if you want. There is so much history to see there."

Bob said, "I know the boys will be interested, and it's after two now. Let's do it in the morning. Are you game, Dave?"

"Sure, bring it on."

Bob went out on deck, and ran into Rick and Jimmy. He asked Rick, "Do you have your things aboard from *Alpha I*?"

"Yes, I'm ready. When are we leaving?"

Bob explained the problem with the remaining stores and Dave's somewhat coerced offer to conduct the tour of el Morrow.

Jimmy asked, "You mean the fort we passed on the way in here?"

"The same."

"Then, when will we be leaving?"

"As originally planned, between two and four in the afternoon tomorrow."

"Rick, would you get the other two and let them know of the change in plans? And get all the blankets you can find so we can keep what perishables we have now cold until we get back. They're going to bring the frozen stuff and rest of the perishables late tomorrow morning. Once we get underway, we'll fire up the ice maker and put everything in the hold. But we don't want to dump frozen harbor water on top of good meat, do we?"

"Not if you plan on my eating it!"

Dan recalled his feelings when Bob had mentioned his thoughts about the St. John's river water coating their food when they first left St. Augustine.

So Dan said, "I'm for seeing the fort. What time will we be going to El Mundo, or whatever that fort is?"

"I don't know. Why don't you check with Captain Dave, but I image it will be early enough to get us down there by the time they open. That's probably around 8:00 A.M."

"OK. Done deal!"

The boys just snacked on Tortilla chips and cans of Diet Pepsi before crashing for the night, but were up well before seven the next morning. Dave Banks was up when Alpha II started to wake up. He was out on the dock smoking one of his "coffin nails", when he noted activity aboard the *II* .Dave said, "Bob is that you makin' all that racket in there?"

"No, Dave, I thought that racket was from you. What's up? If you are ready to tackle the day, I'll get the boys up. I figured if San Juan is between us and the fort, we could probably find a bite of breakfast on the way."

"Yer right there, but just make sure Walt is on a short leash. We've seen what he does after dinner; we don't need to see what he does after breakfast."

The dockside hatch slid open, and Walt stuck his head out, " I heard that. Would you rather I stay back and drop my cookies in the bay right here?"

" No, not on your life. I don't believe the police here could protect you if you contaminated their harbor that way."

It only took a short moment before all were involved in the verbal, good-natured fray. The issue of breakfast was an important issue, since it had been some time that anyone had had a fully satisfying meal. It didn't take long to get the troops out and ready for the day. Banks said that the Fort was about a mile up the road, but breakfast would be about halfway. "If you are all ready, just follow me." The group turned left when they got to Passeo Covadonga. After a few more turns and jogs, the boys didn't know where they were, except the street signs said "Calle De La Forteleza." It was then that they entered Old San Juan. The buildings were old, some dating back to the Spanish occupation in the 1500s. All were to be restored, starting principally with the older, more historic buildings, so that the growth of Puerto Rico, and principally San Juan, would keep its place in history. San Juan played a prominent place in the development of the Central Caribbean, and the group was just beginning to realize that.

Calle de la Forteleza was a wonderland of small shops with jewelers, watchmakers, up scale clothiers, restaurants some rivaling New York's upscale restaurants. On the east side of the street next to a small city park was a fast food breakfast place where they stopped.

Fuelled and rested, after breakfast they continued past the city square, turned up Calle San Juan and continued up the hill, past a small building identified as "Pablo Casals Museum." The deep blue of the ocean opened before them with the remnants of Fort San Christobal interrupting the panorama. To the left of San Cristobal lay the parade grounds and the Fort El Morrow. Because of its strategic position, El Morrow's defenses were strengthened by its Spanish occupiers in 1625 to withstand a threatened Dutch Attack on the island which at the time was considered imminent. By1759, it became apparent to the Spaniards that unless they undertook a massive and prolonged renovation of the defenses of el Morrow and San Christobal a war with Britian, which was then considered imminent, would cause harm and possibly loss of Spanish territorial gains in the Caribbean.

Dan Banks was a virtual library of knowledge, but it was buried in his easygoing manner. To get to the Fort proper, they walked along the parade grounds, then up a long road to the arched entrance to the Fort itself. The Fort was at one time a castle, but had been rehabilitated and fortified. Once a person had passed the gift shop with its histories and photographs, they came upon both the fortifications and the living accommodations of the former garrisons here. The east and northeast walls were populated with gun emplacements and interspersed with ammunition bunkers. On the opposite walls of the Fort appeared to be the living quarters for the troops. On the roof of these facilities there were additional batteries of guns fed by interior passageways, including circular stairways. Dave pontificated continuously throughout the visit, offering a lecture of university proportions on the history of El Morrow. On top of this level in about 1943 the U.S. constructed additional defenses against the Germans in WWII, with state of the art fire controls and watch stations. These were manned but never required during the war, according to Dave.

The tour took them down through Fort San Christobal, where the townspeople lived, with its 18-foot thick walls, and more mortar batteries. By now, it was getting on past noon and Dan said, "Fellows, I think we should be heading back. Besides, I think I've run out of all I know about this place."

The boys' attention was redirected from exploration to anticipation, and their weariness replaced by the spirit of adventure. It had been a long hike, but Bob was wholly in favor of the change. In fact, when they got to the park on Fortaleza, they all opted for a short rest. There were several benches which they readily occupied. The midday bustle was in full swing, and it was relaxing just to sit there and watch the various people making their way through crowds of shoppers. Cavorting across the small park were several small children with no apparent supervision. [But] For noisy exuberance, it was easy to see where the elder Puerto Ricans get their volatility - it is ingrained from their youth!

But, duty did call, and they responded en masse. Their weariness set in during the brief respite in the park, and more so with Dave Banks and Bob. There was a marked reluctance on their part to haul anchor and move on. But, if there was any hesitation evident in any of them it faded into obscurity when they turned the last corner, and saw the Alphas waiting at the dock. Rick asked, "Will we have time for a shower before we pull out?"

"Hop to it," Bob said, for he envisioned the coming weeks without the opportunity of a thorough cleansing except by Providence through the passing of a rainstorm. With the weather they had experienced to date, that did not seem likely. The weather they had so far was not conducive to showering. The small confines of the facilities aboard did nothing to accommodate any of them.

After assurances by Joe that the Ghanaian crew had secured the store, which had all arrived, Bob joined the rest of the boys in line for a final shower, then he headed to Felix's office.

"I guess it's time to say goodbye," Bob said. "We wanted to get started about 4:00 P.M., and it looks like we're on line to make that."

"It's been a pleasure having you and your crew with us these past few days. Please feel free any time you are in the area, drop in and see us. You will always be welcome here."

"Thank you, Felix. If we ever do get back here, we'll do just that, and I'll pass your comments along to the boys. It will mean much more to them coming from a police officer. Maybe it will encourage them to remain on their best behavior just a little longer."

"Well, good luck, and good days to all of you." After the perfunctory handshakes, Bob gave Felix several well-fed Puerto Rican steaks for him and his family.

chapter ten

ANCHORS AWEIGH, AGAIN

The boys checked the stowage of the supplies boarded by the native crew and it was good to go. Joe Shell gave a rundown on what had been placed where, so there would not be any time lost after they left until all was stowed and secured. Bob and Joe started their engines and let them warm up while filters were drained, systems were checked, and lifesaving equipment re-checked. The bilges were not pumped now, rather waiting until they were out of the bay. Joe's ship was in the lead, so Joe did a 180 to head out of the harbor. And when he was clear of the *II*, Bob did the same. Several police were on the dock, Felix among them, so they did not feel a stowaway check was warranted. Joe or Dave blew a salute their way. Bob did the same. And the boys – at least three of them – climbed atop the wheelhouse and Rick on the prow where they could get an unobstructed view of San Juan and el Morrow on their departure. These landmarks were indelibly impressed in their young minds, especially the contentions and emotions of those who wished to invade and conquer the jewel of the Caribbean. Now, it was a move back to normalcy, making sure everything was ship-shape for the long haul. Bob sent Rick down to pump the bilge and to start the seawater icemaker, which took about an hour to generate a useful amount of ice for cooling fish or for preserving foods. After passing el Morrow, Bob called Walt, Dan, and Jimmy down from their vantage point above to redistribute the stores they had boarded in San Juan. Now that they were clear of the harbor and the icemaker was running, it was all right to arrange things as they should be. Bob turned the Furuno depth/fish finder on and pinged the bottom once. It read out 60 fathoms, or 360 feet, which indicated they were past the shelf and it was safe to come about to a more easterly heading. As if on cue, *Alpha I* swung around to 90 degrees. *Alpha II* followed. Fajardo was about four hours ahead. Now, the real test of stamina and resolve began.

The northeast coast of Puerto Rico impressed Bob because of its profusion of palm trees backed by its mountainous spine, notably "El Yunque," a popular park area along the spine. It was primarily low land along the coast with several beautiful beaches interspersed between the palms, but nothing they hadn't seen before. In fact, it reminded him of their home in Largo, with its offshore islands. This created a yearning to call home and it was at that moment he remembered it was time to call, actually past time, because they were in a different time zone now. So he called Rick down from the wheelhouse roof where he had been relaxing with his brothers, asking him if he wanted to talk with Bobi. His response was magnified by the short time it took for Rick to appear at the wheelhouse hatch.

"Is she on the phone now?"

"No, I was just getting ready to call for the patch. Do you want to do it?"

"Sure. Will Bobi be there?"

"I think so, that's the way we'd set this up. At six o'clock all the girls would try to be at our place for the call, and I'm sure those girls would like to talk to each of you."

Rick called the WOM operator in Miami and placed the call from the Alpha II to Bob's home in Largo.

On the third ring, Jo answered, "Hello." Rick paused. He didn't know whether to say, "Mom," or try little subterfuge and ask if Mrs. Roberta Murray was there. But figuring that his mother would recognize his voice anyway, he answered, "Hi, Mom, how are you?"

"Hello, Rick. How are things going with you all? Everything here is fine. Bobi is here, do you want to talk to her?"

"In a minute, but first, we got going about 4:00 P.M. San Juan time this afternoon, and we're coming up on the east coast of Puerto Rico now, at Fajardo." Rick went on to describe his last two days on the *I*, their hike through El Morrow, the conditions on the *I*, and when they ran into the squall line. He was happy now to be on the *II*. All the while Dan was shifting from foot to foot, waiting to talk to Debi. Bob was doing the same mentally. Jimmy came down as well, asking Jo to pass a message on to his parents, which she agreed to do, bringing them up to date. Dan covered the same highlights as did Rick, then it was Bob's turn. The most important thing mentioned was that Jo and Sandi had their reservations out of New York for July 25 on Pan Am! The other reassurance she offered Bob was that she had received a check from Charley.

All in all, the spirits aboard the *II* were high, almost equaling those of their departure from St. Augustine. Bob was pleased with their performance on the first leg. They had: overcome the water problem with no ill effects, weathered a squall line storm at sea, suffered the loss of a hundred pounds of steaks, overcome mechanical failure on both boats, and still displayed the kind of spirit that caused the pride in Bob's heart to boil over. More than that, he was certain that Joe and Dave felt the same way about this ragtag crew.

The VHF awoke him from his reverie: "*Alpha II*, are you there?"

Rick answered, "Where else did you expect us? Come back."

"I just wanted to be sure you are on our tail and to let you know there are subs – U.S. subs – playing around in here sometimes. The U.S. has a naval base on the east end of Puerto Rico, and the navy owns the eastern half of Vieques which is what you see just off your starboard bow. That area is used as a naval firing range, so we're coming to port about 30 degrees. That should keep us clear of any plans they haven't told us about. Once, I was coming through here and a sub surfaced close in to us.

"Thanks Joe. I'll tell Dad."

"No need Rick, I heard it all."

Bob came up and flipped the switch on the Furuno. The bottom here was fairly uniform, punctuated with rock outcroppings that drove the depth finder to less than 20 fathoms. That was not a depth that posed any concern. Their two boats only drew about 8.5 feet of water, or a little over 1 fathom.

In the meantime, Joe had altered his course to parallel St. Thomas on a more easterly heading. The lights of Charlotte Amalie were all ablaze, with lights of the airport blending in behind the city. In the gathering dusk one could still see the outline of the mountains behind the city. Not tall mountains, mind you, but a striking accent in the evening twilight. St. Thomas reminded Bob of a tadpole looking east, with Charlotte Amalie situated at the joint between the body and the tail. They had to swing to the south to sail around the distended belly of the tadpole, and then resumed the heading that would carry them past the island of St. John. The night was a chamber of commerce's delight, no wind except the little breeze the *II* generated as it glided, almost silently it seemed, through the easy swells. And the sky was an astronomer's delight. Once you get away from any major land mass and its contributing pollution, dust, and yes, lights – lights can be a pollutant as well to mar the beauty of the night. When he climbed to the top of the wheelhouse planning to recline in the life raft and watch for shooting stars and an occasional satellite overhead, he found Rick already had had the same thought. Rick graciously moved over so Bob had a place to stretch out on the raft.

Bob had no more than gotten comfortable, when Rick said, "Look, there's one! See, it's almost directly overhead, heading southeasterly, I think."

"Yes, I see it. Not very bright, is it?"

"Well, your eyes will adjust. When I first came up top, I was beginning to think there no satellites out tonight. Then I started seeing them. They must have been there all the time, but I wasn't seeing them."
Excusing himself, Rick said," Dad, I've got to be up in four hours or so, so I'd better get some shuteye now, or that nasty old sun will be giving me a headache I don't want when I'm driving straight into it."

"OK, Rick, happy dreams." Bob watched the satellites for an indeterminate period, then caught himself dozing, as he woke to chills and shivering. (That's the other thing they all learned on this trip. On the open sea, it can get uncomfortably cold when the sun goes down and there are no land masses nearby to cast off the heat stored up during the day.) Consequently, they had all brought light jackets and sweatshirts, shorts and sweatpants, and would be happy to have them before this trip was over. That was in addition to their foul weather gear. Their destination was only 5 degrees north of the equator. None of them figured on cold weather in that neighborhood, but at the suggestion of both Joe and Dave, they had outfitted themselves satisfactorily. The sea water temperature was constant at about 58 degrees F.

Bob decided enough was enough, cast a glance around him, and noting the distant lights of St. John, clambered down from his perch. The carpet above was festooned with a wealth of diamonds. Some appeared so close you felt a handful was almost within your grasp. That carpet, so immense, so beautiful, did more to obscure the satellite display than anything else Bob could think of. But, everything comes with a price, and the price here was to be exacted in the morning. He had only about eight hours before he was due to be on duty again, so he bade Walt and Jimmy in the wheelhouse good night and descended into his private "digs". Of the two left in the wheelhouse, one was to be at the helm, following Joe, and the other was to be checking systems and housekeeping. Bob wasn't sure which was which, but figured if they knew, that's all that mattered. He bid them both good night again and descended the steps to his cabin. One of those latent thoughts that he had earlier filed away in the recesses of the mind popped to the front. He stooped to turn on the chart table lamp, then reviewed the chart looking for the area of "unexploded ordinance". They were well clear of it. Satisfied, he kicked off his shoes and stretched out on his bunk.

When Bob awoke, they were snaking their way through the islands south of Tortolla, being greeted by a flotilla of white sails, some highlighted by a single diagonal stripe of either blue, red, or yellow. Since these were under sail, the Alphas were obliged to give way to them. Fortunately, they were strung out for about a mile or better along a prescribed course marked by buoys. This apparently was not a competition that made any reporting system, consequently notices such as are available to airborne flight crews in the form of NOTAMS (Notices To Airmen) were not issued, and *Alpha II's* only information as to what was going on was the VHF contact with Joe or Dave. Joe suggested that this was more of a spontaneous affair starting out off Peter Island, an Amway resort and used to entertain their top distributors. But Walt was still up, already figuring who he could contact to fill in vacancies in the crew log on one of these ships, and it didn't have to be here in the Caribbean. It could be right there in Clearwater, and he did know some boat owners with boats docked near their homes. Besides, his dad was acquainted with many owners at Clearwater Marina where Bob and Charley had kept the Sea Esta. Walt filed a mental note to talk it over with his dad when this trip was over.

This display of disposable income was apparently a regular well-intentioned race, performed on weekends throughout the summer honing the racing skills of the owners and/ or captains of the various boats.

Neither Joe nor Dave was interested in what the armada's intentions were. Joe's only interest was to get clear of this impediment to their progress, but Dave had two interests: one was to get clear, and the other was to ogle his mermaid. He seemed to be handling that job very well. There were many crewmember candidates aboard those ships who could pass for candidates to be mermaids.

The plan for navigating the voyage was for Joe, who had the only sextant aboard either of the Alphas to take the noon (Greenwich) sun shot and determine their position by referencing the solar charts. All were comfortable with the accuracy of the instrument, having had several occasions en route to San Juan to cross check against both radio aids and visual sightings. The lat-longs (latitude/longitude) were determined and coordinated between the boats by VHF and found to be consistently accurate.

This was an exercise repeated earlier at St. Augustine, reassuring all that the sextant had not been subject to any abuse that would render it inaccurate. The sun shot is predicated on the dual rotations - both the earth on its axis, and of the earth around the sun. The position of any point on the earth can be determined by the relative position of a celestial body with respect to the horizon at a time certain. A noon shot is the most common sight taken and was the choice of these mariners, but it is not the only one. The key to any determination was the alignment of the mirrors. Even a one-degree error could result in a vast difference in the viewer's position, and in unmarked area of underwater obstructions could have disastrous consequences. In practice, a sight is generally accurate to within about 0.2 degrees, or about 400 yards. A nautical mile is defined as 1852 meters, or one minute of angle on the globe. Most experienced navigators, with two sights and the correct time within a second, can achieve an accuracy of less than 1.5 nm. In most instances, that's close enough to see a city or locate a harbor. The time of day the sight is taken is also critical, since the earth turns about 15 degrees an hour, and must be accounted for in reducing the sight to an earthly result or location. This nomally is accounted for in the *Nautical Almanac*, a collection of tables by which the navigator can reduce the raw sighting data to a latitude/longitude position on his chart.

They had joined the armada for a short while to facilitate the crossing of paths to the east. The armada continued to the south although there were many greetings hailed back and forth by this gang of weekend pirates, all in good taste. Several of the sailboats making up the armada were crewed by women, and the boys spied Dave on the foredeck of *Alpha I* with his binoculars looking for his mermaid, of course. The boys were caught up in the significance of the search, so with a single voice they all headed for the wheelhouse to lay claim to the binocs aboard. The resulting contest generated nothing more than bruised egos, and a truce was reached with an agreement to share. This, however, was often punctuated by an accuser claiming that the binoculars were being held by one person too long. In most cases it appeared the accusation was just.

.

After the transition, the boys watched the objects of their affections glide slowly to the rear and gradually disappear over the horizon. Walt said, "Boy, those girls were sure having fun!"

Someone said, "Don't you wish you were with them instead of here?"

"Well, they showed a lot more life than this set of deadheads!"

Dan said, "When do you want to study?"

This seemed to be a prime time to settle the issue, since everyone was up and awake right then, so Bob said," I've been thinking about that. We've been gone a little over a week, and haven't had an open Bible study with everyone present yet. Everyone is usually up for supper, such as it is, so what would you say to right after supper, about seven o'clock? And for the initial subjects, why don't we start with the references to the sea in the scriptures? The sea was very prominent in Jesus' ministry in many ways, wasn't it?"

"Yeah, that would keep us from knocking each other's block off!"

"Are any of you at that point yet, Dan?"

"No, Dad. That was just a figure of speech."

"Well, I would hope so. Who's in the barrel after supper?"

Rick said he thought he was, along with Walt. Bob and Jimmy were to follow at midnight.

Dan was encouraged to get busy rustling up something for the crew to eat, and said, "Lunch comes before supper, usually, doesn't it? Well, I'd planned something a little special for dinner, so I thought we could have cold cereal and beef jerky for lunch if that's OK with everyone." There was no apparent dissention, so Dan hustled back to get the jerky and cereal and milk set up.

Rick raised a point, "Hey, Dan, what is this something special you've got in mind for tonight?"

"Well, I'd rather it be a surprise."

It probably will be. Just pray that it won't be the kind of surprise we will be paying for in the weeks ahead!"

"All right, knock it off. In fact why don't you guys get a little sunshine, or jog around the block. It gets a little crowded in here, and I want to get Dave on the horn."

"*Alpha I, Alpha II.* Dave, come back."

"This is Dave, Bob. Whatcha got?"

"Dave, what was that island you were talking about before we left St. Augustine? That was somewhere in the eastern Caribbean, wasn't it?"

"You got that right. It's St. Bartholomey, St. Bart's for short."

"When do we come up on that one?"

"We got to come around St. Maarten first, then it's just a stones throw from there, but maybe not 'til morning. From there, it's straight to Barbuda, and straight on to Africa."

"Don't know if you've studied up on St. Maarten, but it has two very different cultures. The southern part of the island is Dutch, while the north is definitely French. The buildings on the French side have a definite French accent to them, and many of the Dutch buildings reflect the architecture seen in Amsterdam. Now you know more than most people know about St. Maarten, so you boys can dazzle your classmates with your knowledge."

"Dave, I thank you. No, I haven't studied up on any of these islands, and haven't as yet flown into any of them, but I do have an opportunity when we get back from this trip to set up a commuter airline out of San Juan primarily to Dominica. And who knows, service could spill over into other islands as well."

"OK, I'm out. Dan said earlier that he had something special planned for dinner tonight and I'd like to get an idea of what he's planning to feed us before I run completely out of options. Good night, Dave."

"Good night, Bob."

To Rick, who had come forward in somewhat early anticipation of his shift he said," I'm going aft to talk to Dan. I'm curious about this surprise we're going to be fed tonight. We've had enough diarrhea aboard for a couple of cruises so far."

Bob set the autopilot and stepped out of the starboard hatch, intending to stop by the galley and query Dan, when Jimmy rounded the corner from the engine room hatch. Bob asked him, "All OK below?"

"Yes sir. Bilges are almost dry; at least I couldn't get any more water out of them. The engine did take some oil, though. About a half gallon is all."

"Go up in the wheelhouse and enter that in the engine log with the date and time you added it. And while you're up there, you can stand by the wheel for a while. If we change course at all, Joe or Dave will call on the VHF first. I'll be on the aft deck for a bit after I talk to Dan."

"Yessir."

The night was cool, and the sun was setting. Bob wondered why it set so late. He didn't figure it was because they were dropping down toward the equator, but that was the only explanation he could think of. Joe had solar tables in the almanac. Bob would call him later and pick up the sunset and sunrise times. They had not checked on those since San Juan. He slid the galley hatch open and quietly called to Dan, who came outside. Bob said, "Dan, what's this chef's special you are cooking up for us tonight?"

"Well, Dad, some of the boys talked it over and we felt it would be better served for breakfast. I was going to make a batch of donuts. Since we make fairly good coffee now, I felt the donuts would go good with it, so for tonight you have your choice between cold cereal and snacks."

"Such a choice!"

"Say, Dad, did I tell you? It looks like you are losing a little weight!"

"Well, I think the cuisine aboard may be one explanation for that."

"Don't knock it. I know how hard you have tried to lose a little. Now that it appears you are doing it. Be happy!"

"I'm going back aft to see the famed green flash. From what they tell me, this is perfect weather for it. Want to come?"

"Sure."

"Was anyone else up in there?"

"No, but I think Walt was awake. I put a pot of coffee on and made a little noise, so he asked me –
no, he told me – to keep it down so he could sleep."

chapter eleven

GREEN FLASH

"OK, let's see what this flash is all about. If it is something to behold, Walt will get another chance before we get to Tema. If it isn't and we got him up for essentially nothing, we would probably hear about it forever."

They heard the VHF come to life. Dave was on the horn advising any who were listening that they might have an opportunity to witness the famed "green flash". The hatch slid open, and Jimmy appeared with the news, so he joined Bob and Dan, and the three of them made their way to the aft rail. None of them knew what the green flash was; consequently, they imagined a wide variety of wonders from fireworks to a sky filled with emerald green light, although Bob was aware that it could only be seen if a person was on an island or a boat with open sea between them and the setting sun. The curvature of the earth acts as a lens, much the same was a prism separates light into the various colors of the spectrum.

Bob continued, "The amazing characteristics of this interaction between the earth and its atmosphere are only part of the story. You are beginning to see another part. That is the magnification of celestial objects such as the sun and the moon, as is now starting to show as the earth ducks behind its atmosphere."

It was true. The sun, at noonday, was a nickel-sized object in a cloudless setting and was now growing to silver dollar size and beyond! The golden orb had descended to the horizon and appeared stuck like a beach ball on a seal's nose, then gradually slipped into obscurity for another day.

The sun slid silently into a watery grave, now only half visible above the horizon.

From that point, it seemed reluctant to make the plunge, slowing ever so slightly in its downward path until just a chord-like sliver remained as evidence of the grandeur it had exhibited while in full bloom.

Three pairs of eyes were fixed on or near the retreating sun, and three minds attempted to decipher what was to be next, and when. As it continued lower and lower, it reminded them of a round cake cut in vertical slices from the center outward, each slice growing slimmer, closer to the ultimate – the slice with the most icing. So it was with the setting of the sun. But the green flash did not appear at that moment. No, the green flash occurs when the last bit of icing was licked clean. And it only lasts for an instant. Blink, and you may have missed it. But the three aboard the *Alpha II* were not to be the victims of inattention. No, they had waited far too long that they could not wait just a few seconds longer.

The sun's fiery tendrils licked the last of the icing, and in the same instant, there was the unmistakable emerald green flash. It was anticlimactic. There was no rolling thunder, no open heavens, and no Fourth of July fireworks, but there was the green flash, a salute to a sun that offered so much to world largely devoid of understanding.

"*Alpha II, Alpha I*, Come back." Three pairs of bare feet sprinted toward the wheelhouse. Jimmy won.

"*Alpha II* here, come back."

"Who's that? Jimmy? Did you get to see the flash?"

"Yes, there were only three of us up then, but we all saw it. Wasn't much to it, was there?"

"Well, I guess if you're talking to someone who has never seen it, you could make a pretty entertaining story about it, don't you think? And afore I forget, the reason I called was to give you guys a heads up on an upcoming course change. In about two to three hours we will be coming around St. Bart's, and will be cutting 15 to 20 degrees to starboard. Let Bob, or whoever will be on the helm, know."

"I'm right here, and heard it all. What's the reason for the course change?"

"Oh, no real reason. By then it will be daylight again, and we should be rounding the north coast of St. Bart's then tooling down the east coast of St. Bart's, where the topless fishes play."

"Dave, are you still looking for those mermaids?"

"Every chance I get!"

"Dave, do you still believe in the tooth fairy or Santa Claus, maybe?"

They had a good laugh over Dave and his mermaids. You could hear the smile in Dave's voice as he said, "Good night, Bob. Good night, boys."

"Happy dreams, Dave."

Bob went to his cabin and raised WOO, New York. He asked to be patched through to his home in Largo. He figured he was a little late, but felt the girls may have started talking. In that case, there's no telling when they'd quit.

At his house, the girls had all gone home, realizing the time difference was working against them. They consoled themselves by this thought, *Six P.M. here is probably noon or 1 o'clock to them now, so maybe they thought it was just too late to reach us. No, that's wrong. When six P.M. rolls around here, it's midnight or later out there. We'll ask them about it tomorrow."*

So the boys, too, went to bed unfulfilled. But Bob placed a call to Charley, while he had WOO on the line. Charley answered on the first ring. Bob said," Hi Charley, Glad I caught you before your bedtime. Bob gave him a position report, details of their fuelling experience in San Juan, a rundown on the mis-rigged turnbuckle incident, and Desco's prompt attention to the Kohler mechanical problem, including their "manifold coffee." The latter brought a chuckle out of Charley, with the observation that they were almost exactly where they figured to be at that time. Charley asked Bob to pass his best wishes off to Joe and Dave and the boys, which Bob agreed to do.

About 7:30 in the morning, they rounded the northeast coast of St. Bart's, to an improbable scene. Ahead lay a wide expanse of beach, with airplanes - albeit small commuter types, Brittian-Norman Islanders, some twin engined Cessnas, and an occasional DeHaviland Twin Otter, taking off out of the mountain and heading out to sea. As they drew closer Bob got a clearer picture of what was going on. The airport at St Bart's was nestled perpendicular to the ridge that ran north/south forming a spine, so aircraft landing came in low over the spine, cut their power and literally glided down the slope of the mountain, hopped over the airport fence and the road, and landed on the down-sloping runway. The trick appeared to be to navigate the various elements of the approach, land, and stop before you got a salt water wash job, courtesy of the St. Bart's chamber of commerce.

chapter twelve

THE MERMAID HUNTER

The airport, its location, and its associated problems were intriguing to Bob. Not so with Dave on *Alpha I.* He was still looking for his mermaids, for coming up on their starboard side was the expanse of beach they had seen earlier, now being populated with people of every form and shape. Apparently they were of every nationality. There were, like the coconuts of musical fame, big ones, small ones, some as big as your head. They all wondered what Dave would do if the one that occupied his mind were to be found on the isle of St. Bart's sometime in July, or maybe in St. Maarten, or in some other topless haven in the world. Today, he would have to be satisfied with the knowledge that she truly existed. They were chugging along about 50 to 100 yards off shore, a bit too far for a swim, and beyond Dave's capability to walk over. So they came to the conclusion that Dave would have to be satisfied with the knowledge that she truly existed. But one thing was certain. Dave would not give up. With Dave, the hunt is the thing. Like the hunter who spends his life and energy searching for the trophy Dall sheep, or the fisherman looking for the trophy bass or walleye. Dave knew his trophy was still out there, but it hadn't dawned on him what to do if he found her.

"*Alpha II, Alpha I,* we're coming to port to 110 degrees. Acknowledge." That was Joe. Dave had not given up his watchdog characteristics.

"Roger. Coming to 110 degrees, Joe."

As they made the course correction, they saw a single object about 20 points off the starboard bow. It looked like a tall, a very tall ship coming toward them. It reminded Rick of a destroyer or similar naval vessel. "What's that ahead of us?" he asked. "It looks like it's coming right towards us."

Dave was back on the horn, "Well fellers that ain't gonna hurt us none, unless we hit it 'cause it ain't going anywhere. That's Redondo Rock, one of the abnormalities that make life in the Caribbean interesting. But, not to worry, it's two or three hours ahead if we was to head straight for it, which we ain't gonna do! That rock is something over 200 feet high, so it can be seen for quite a distance – on a clear day, that is. Does make you wonder sometimes, though, how many other 'abnormalities' there are out here that didn't quite make it to the surface. But, most of them have been charted by now. At least we hope so."

Everyone was up now, eagerly awaiting Dan's surprise breakfast dish. Well, not so eagerly, actually. The boys were hungry, and the talk of Dan's special did nothing to satisfy it.

Bob and Jimmy clambered on top of the wheelhouse to greet the sun. Dan was in the galley concocting his special and the other two boys were on the aft deck enjoying the cool breeze generated by the passing of the ship at its rated speed of just less than 10 knots. All were amazed at their good fortune with the weather. Except for the one squall line en route to San Juan, they had no adverse weather, even now, heading into the birthplace of many of the northern hemisphere's most violent storms. But, the voyage wasn't over. They had not yet reached their halfway point.

Dan appeared at the galley hatch, a bit crestfallen. Something was not right. Rick, who had been on the helm asked, "Dan, what's wrong? Are you all right?"

"Yes I'm OK, but there's something wrong with the donuts. They didn't rise."

The race to the galley was won by Rick who found himself confronted with a platter of fifty-cent sized animal crackers weighing in at about a quarter pound apiece. They were harder than bricks and about as tasty. Walt commented, "These would make good sinkers for the fishing gear we brought on board!"

"Fishing gear! We forgot about that!" The rest of the crew chimed in, with the same refrain. So another activity was born. Later that day they ran into a school of flying fish, some twenty landing on the aft deck. The boys ran for a bucket, looped a line around its bail and after hauling in a load of sea water over the aft rail, started dumping flying fish in it. What they failed to realize was that flying fish found their way on to the deck, first by leaping into the air and then using their fins to glide for prodigious distances. For a while, the boys seemed to stay ahead of the mass, but the law of recovery eventually caught up with them. The law of recovery, simply stated, is that when two go into the bucket, three leave. One could easily see frustration setting in among them. But when they saw what was happening, they devised a strategy to stay ahead of the game. A free tarp was employed to cover the bucket between deposits.

The fishing gear consisted of a #2 and a #4 weight as sinkers, diving planes to control the depth they would be fishing, stainless steel leaders, and a variety of hooks, from large to extra large. They had high hopes. When Dave Banks sailed on *Alpha II* to San Juan, he discouraged the boys in their fishing activities, saying, "How will you land the whale you're fishing for?" So the boys just filed Dave's comments away for some time in the future. Boredom, with a little tedium mixed in hastened the process, but the future is now! They got everything ready, but deferred casting the first hook. *Alpha I* was still among islands, with the ever watchful Dave aboard as lookout, and as far as the boys were concerned, there may have been another St. Bart's among those islands remaining to be discovered, including Antigua and Barbuda.

Dan had an idea of how to redeem himself from the donut fiasco. The more he gazed upon the flying fish, the more the similarity he noticed between them and the smelt they used to dip from the Columbia and the Cowlitz Rivers in Washington State. So Dan busied himself for the afternoon by taking three or four reasonable specimens out of the bucket and de-finned and gutted them. He then stole almost silently into the galley and prepared them as though they were smelt. His only error was in not scaling them, for while he was frying the scales curled up. But he had found a new delight to tease the palates on board. Dan took one, and outside of a few scales, it was considered a victory!

Dan took the remaining fish forward and shared them with Rick, Walt, and Jimmy. Bob got a piece of Rick's. They agreed Dan had now vindicated himself. They set about to create a fish trap. Walt went below and brought up a trouble light from the forepeak, which was rigged by hanging the light from the net cable aft of the winch. The power cord was strung through the hatch in the head and plugged in to 110v AC current. Someone said it appeared the fish that came aboard the other day came from aft as if they were following the craft. All agreed, and it was decided that the light should be placed high and as far aft as possible.

Their present course would take them just south of Barbuda, a low cut jewel standing as a silent guardian over the Antilles north of Antigua, which was well within view to the south. Barbuda had its own attraction to these neophyte sailors. Two small, two-man pram-type vessels, under sail crossed their paths heading, it seemed, for somewhere certain, but they offered no outward clues as to where that somewhere might be. It reminded Bob of the natives in Alaska that would leave their village on a two week walrus or seal hunting expedition with only their sled and dogs to accompany them. After zigzagging over the ice shelf for that time, the hunt generally successful, they would turn their dogs toward home, and run a bee-line course back to the village. The natives in Polynesia possess much the same navigational talents depending on water currents, winds, and temperature, to give an indication of where they are. They always appeared to arrive home at last, and pretty much on schedule. They all seemed to be cut from the same cloth while navigating on water, frozen or not.

Having poked all the fun at Dan that they could think of at the moment, Bob included, the "donuts" were dumped overboard under last rites for any seagoing creatures that might chance upon them and be unfortunate enough to consume one or more. The last barb hurled at Dan was that such an animal, or fish in this case, was certain to be a bottom feeder by reason of all the weight in its belly.

Another regatta was underway out of Antigua which was associated with its Halycon Festival. These were more magnificent craft than those out of Tortolla/ Peter Island. Most were under sail, but there were a few powered boats in the armada. Of the sailboats there were several that appeared longer than the *Alpha's* 73 feet, at an estimated cost of well into the millions of dollars. They had never before seen such a display of discretionary dollars on the loose! Of the few powerboats, they, too were amply represented in the discretionary dollar sweepstakes. One of these craft had two lighters, one on each side of the aft deck at the aft rail. Nestled between them sat a seaplane, a Husky on floats with an extensible overhead crane on rails for both launching and recovery of the aircraft.

Antigua was a bustling port with deep water facilities. It contrasted with Barbuda, a sleepy little wisp of an island, but well known in the Caribbean for its quiet ambience, and for its lack of modern tourist facilities. It ties with Dominica as the islands that if Columbus were ever to revisit the area, they would be the only islands he would recognize. Barbuda's only access, as with many Caribbean islands, was by boat or by air, for it has a small airstrip – so small, it was as if they had taken a small airstrip, dipped it in the water several times, and hung the shrunken version out in the Caribbean sun to dry.

Dinner that night was courtesy of Dinty Moore, a beef stew judged locally to be outstanding, particularly when compared to Dan's breakfast contribution of the morning. The night was reminiscent of the typical tropical nights seen on television, the kind that travel agents are most familiar with by reason of their brochures, and not necessarily by reason of experience. They waved goodbye to Barbuda and set about their daily routines, which had changed slightly over the past day. They were now looking ahead to a continuous period of open sea, with no service stations in sight. That was a real consideration for Bob, when he gave thought to traveling cross country with this gang, their fifteen-year-old-sister, and his wife. Bob had not thought about Jo's rejection of his offer to accompany them on this venture since they departed St. Augustine. Now, he thought what a mistake that would have been, thinking of the storm they weathered and the mechanical problems they faced, all of which turned out well. But not with women aboard (he probably would have had to bring his daughter along as well). No, in this setting, the boys were free to find their own way in the world, to recognize the differences they can make all by themselves. They learned to accept responsibility for their actions as well as those omissions by others, when their own inaction contributed to the problem.

Bob had determined that a different schedule would be more advantageous for him in dealing with his daily records. The shifts were set as before, midnight to 6:00 A.M. as the first shift, and the second from six 'til noon, and so on through the twenty-four hour cycle. Bob took the second shift both for efficiency and convenience. The change was to take place over the next day, so all affected by the change hit the sack early, Bob included.

chapter thirteen

FIRE ON BOARD!

At two in the morning, acrid fumes escaping from the engine room seeped upward through the weep holes in the floor of Bob's cabin, invading his sanctuary.

"FIRE!" he shouted as he jumped from his bunk.

His shout startled Walt, who was on the helm. Bob burst into the wheelhouse, saying "Walt, get the boys up, we've got a fire down below, then get back here!"

By now, the fumes were easily distinguished as burning insulation throughout the ship.

Bob cut the circuit breakers to all AC power , but left the battery circuit live for VHF communications and emergency lighting. He called, "*Alpha I, Alpha I, Alpha II.* Come back!" There was urgency in his voice.

"*Alpha II*, This is Joe. What's up?"

"Joe, don't get too far away. We've got a fire down below somewhere. It smells like electrical insulation burning!"

"Hang on, we'll be right over."

"Thanks, Joe." "Walt, open the forward hatch a bit and see how much smoke you can see down there. Here, better take this flashlight, If there is no smoke or just light smoke, go back and open the rear hatch, but just a crack at first. If it is a fire in flammable materials it could blossom up when fresh air gets to it. Be careful.

Same thing as up front. If there is little or no smoke and you can get down there, go on down and shut the Kohler down. I've already pulled the breakers. On your way back, stick your head in and make sure the rest are getting up."

But Walt was already on the forepeak, checking for smoke below. He then ran to the galley hatch to make sure they were all moving, then sped off to the engine room hatch. Rick and Jimmy were the first to show in the wheelhouse, Jimmy sharing duty with Walt, but had been on the aft deck checking security of the deck equipment.

As Walt descended to the engine room, his eyes started to burn, and his throat tightened. It was like he had gotten soap in his eyes. They were now burning and it was getting difficult to breathe. Walt began to choke a little. He rubbed his eyes but that didn't help - in fact, it made things worse. He was getting miserable, blinking more often to keep his eyes moist, which was the greater help.

Rick said, "Did Walt say we had a fire?"

"We may have. I was **awakened** by the smell of insulation burning. The smoke was apparently coming in through the weep holes in the flooring. I've already contacted Joe who is coming over to lend a hand, if necessary. Walt is below trying to find out where that smoke was coming from. I don't like the idea that he is below in a smoke-filled room alone. Rick, take this flashlight and go below to check on him, please."

As Rick descended the engine room stairs he could see the beam from Walt's flashlight flitting back and forth forward of the Cat engine. Rick began to feel the effects of the smoke as he made his way to where Walt was. He called out, "Walt, find anything?"

"I think so. Come here."

Rick made his way forward until he was right behind Walt. Walt shone his light on the two-inch Kohler exhaust which was insulated with asbestos to about six feet above the engine room deck, then went horizontally through the hull on the port side above the waterline. But Walt was not shining his light on the overhead exhaust run. He was shining it about twelve inches above its connection to the engine.

"See that burned insulation?"

"Yes."

"Well, when we repaired this unit in San Juan, there was no indication of excess heat or anything out of the ordinary then. As soon a it cools a little I'm going to strip this insulation jacket off and see what's under there."

Walt split the jacket and removed it to allow the area to cool faster. As it was removed, he saw what appeared to be a pinhole in the exhaust stack, about the size of the lead for a Scripto pencil, or 7mm. But the sleeve he removed from the Kohler exhaust showed definite stains from the heat it had been subjected to. The hole was in the weld between the attach flange and the exhaust pipe. Walt went topside, poured himself a cup of coffee and went forward to report his finding to Bob while the pipe cooled.

Joe announced his presence with two blasts of his horn, and a glance outside showed Bob that Joe was only bout 20 yards to starboard, so Bob answered him with a toot of his own. Walt then went on to explain what he felt was the problem. Walt told him that the insulation had been stripped back, and it would probably be cool enough to devise a fix in fifteen or twenty minutes.

Author's note: The reader may question why it seems these two boats are always playing to the starboard of the other. That is because there were two personnel hatches on the starboard side, the galley/ crew quarter hatch and the wheelhouse hatch, and only a wheelhouse hatch on the port side. So you are more likely to get a real live body to answer you on the starboard than on the port, particularly if the one is on autopilot and the helmsman is attending to an emergency or other problem.

Bob asked if Walt was sure. Walt said, "I can't be sure until we can repair it, and fire it up to see if that corrects the problem."

"How will you fix it?"

"I don't know yet, but I'll think of something."

There's the power of positive thinking in action!

"I'm sure you will. Just keep me up-to-date. You think then that it's OK to load the DC bus to bring the battery power back online?"

"Yes. That pinhole was the only thing I've found, but like I said, I can't be sure 'til we give it a good test."

"I'm going to bring Joe up to speed."

So he contacted Joe on *Alpha I* and explained what they had found, and that as soon as the Kohler had cooled, Walt was going to attempt a repair. Their main power had been unaffected, so Bob suggested that they keep on for Africa. Their DC power was supplied by generators on the Cats, only their AC power was affected, which meant back to the manifold for coffee and no cooking or refrigeration, until Walt worked one of his wonders.

Walt went back below, and rummaged round in the spares storage area in the forepeak. He found a tube of high temperature gasket material and a few screws. He then went back to the Kohler, cut a small section off his own leather belt, bore a small hole in it, smeared it with the high temp gasket material and screwed it in place on the exhaust pipe. When the material was set, he started the Kohler. There were no indications that this was a jury-rigged repair. Walt left the section of insulation off that he had removed, concerned about the heat buildup from the Kohler exhaust if there was insulation keeping the heat in. He went back topside and reported as far as he knew now, the Kohler repair was done and was holding. Bob told Walt, "That was a good job, Walt. You've earned your keep for this trip. Incidentally, can we hang the AC power back on line? I was not really looking forward to another couple of weeks without cooking or refrigeration and instant coffee off the manifold!"

"Sure, bring it back on line. That should pull a load on it and give us an indication of how effective the fix is and if it is holding that much sooner".
"Yeah, I wasn't really looking forward to a repeat of our second day out either."

"Perhaps that is what inspired you!"

"Maybe. I don't care. It's holding so far. That's all that matters, right?"

"Right."

The AC breakers were closed, and at least for the time being, all was back to normal. The range and refrigerator were tried and they worked! [**And**] The air conditioning units cut in with their slight homespun buzz of reassurance.

It made a long day for most of them, with sleep a precious commodity that was only available in short and elusive spurts. [So]{ **Cut**} Plan 'B' was employed, whereby a body rested as long as was necessary, and the slack was taken up by volunteers who felt they had sufficient rest. Bob and Rick placed themselves in this latter group.

Therefore the duty assignments became very scrambled for a day after their "fire". Dan offered to take the helm for two to four hours, and let those who worked through the night sleep it off. Joe seemed very relieved and told Walt that he had the makings of an honest-to-goodness seaman.

JIMMY WHITE ON WATCH : All's quiet this day!

Walt got his jollies by watching Joe and Dave come about to track again on the 110 degree course. Bob slept until after four P.M. His first thought on awaking was of the Kohler repair. The second was whether they had missed their call time to the States. Walt had awakened an hour before with the same question on his mind, and had been up and checked the Kohler. It was still purring along, with no squeaks or other spurious noises coming forth. Best of all, the repair to the exhaust was doing fine.

That evening the routine that they had missed was reinstated, and Bob called Joe to get their noon position. Satisfied that their progress of 246 nautical miles was in line with their planned progress, he climbed atop the wheelhouse to enjoy the setting of the sun, a little over an hour away.

Dan had brought four packages of frozen chicken out of the fishhold for dinner, augmenting it with boiled rice and beans. The beans had been soaking even when they had the Kohler problem. Dan said he was following Joe's recipe for rice and beans and they honestly said it was one of the better meals they had on the voyage, which lifted Dan's spirits off the charts. He also said they had taken a good number of flying fish aboard last night but everyone had been tied up in knots that they failed to save any to eat. They were encouraged by the fact that their fish trap had apparently worked, so they were bound to try it again. That night they set the single bulb lure swaying over the aft deck again. All hands that could went to sleep counting flying fishes – or maybe they were counting frying fishes.

In the nightly call home, Bob described the excitement of the day, and each of the boys in turn embellished the feats of Walt a little more. Cindy was there, and Walt, while talking to her played down his part in the repair process, but all aboard agreed that it took a bit of ingenuity to devise the repair, considering the limited resources he had to work with and keeping the delivery on course. If it had not happened, they would have had to return to Antigua - with no firm date for completion of those repairs - remove the insulation and re-weld the leaking joint. It probably would have been in the neighborhood of one or two days. But the underlying problem was, what the Ghanaians would think of a ship that was designed and built to fish for a month on the sea, yet couldn't make it for half a month on its delivery voyage. Or, a new ship that couldn't maintain a schedule. It's something to consider. But, the general feeling aboard *Alpha II* was, "That is all behind us now."

The boys took advantage of the fact that all were up and, for the most part, awake. After the fire experience, they had a more realistic concept of their mortality, so Rick and Dan asked Bob, "Dad, can we have that Bible study you talked about yesterday, or the day before?"

"Certainly. Get the other boys and bring your books."

The five of them assembled in the wheelhouse, with the heading locked in the autopilot. The autopilot was a poor man's version of a heading controller, in that it would bracket the desired course and permit the boat's heading to swing about 5 degrees either side of the selected course. But on average, if they wanted a 110-degree track, after, say, an hour, they would be less than a half mile off of the course line. It, too, was a hunter, like Dave – it never lost sight of its goal.

The five of them assembled in the wheelhouse with scriptural references to the sea as a subject. It was obvious from their thoughts and comments that they had been reading and thinking about what was read. Rick and Bob had been reading in Psalms 107:23-30. Psalm 107:27 reads: "They reel to and fro, and stagger like a drunken man, and are at their wit's end." Verse 30 says: "Then they are glad, because they be quiet; so He bringeth them to their desired Haven". That Psalm was very comforting to them for the balance of their journey, especially after their latest fright. They had numerous additional thoughts, the details of which by reason of time (and the author's aging memory) have been lost - at least temporarily.

The VHF woke from its slumber. Joe said, "It looks like tomorrow is going to be a beautiful day and if so, we wondered if we could trade some reading material. We've gone through all we have."
The *Alpha II* crew took a quick count among themselves. Then Bob said, "Joe, what was here to read has either already been read, or it is not fit to read, but you're welcome to it. But just how do you plan to make this transfer?"

"We will talk about it in the morning. Just be assured that transfers like this are commonplace, but let's make sure we have calm seas in the morning and we'll go through the exercise then."

"OK. Catch you in the morning. Say, if they are so commonplace, why didn't we use the transfer to save some of those steaks? They could have been put in your ice area."

"You know, you have a good point. I'll file that away for the next time."

The night was one of those glorious evenings, beautiful sunset that reminded Bob of the old adage, *Red at night, sailor's delight. Red in the morning, sailors take warning.* The sunset was brilliant in various hues – predominantly reds, but also including orange and yellow.

The morning broke bright and clear, the sea was calm, in fact there were very few swells to disturb the peacefulness. Almost automatically, Bob wondered how the weather was back in Largo. Inwardly, he hoped they had a day like this to enjoy. He surmised he would have to wait until evening to find out.

Dan came trotting up saying, "We've got a few fish back here. Anyone want to help scale them?" All three boys headed aft to help gather them but Bob put a temporary halt to the operation reminding them of the transfer of reading materials.

Dave came up on the VHF. "You guys awake yet?"

"Hey! Give us a break! It's almost noon, somewhere. What gave you the impression we weren't paying attention to business?"

""Just the zigzag track you're leaving behind you."

Bob ducked outside because the engine stack would not let him see straight behind them. The stack and the rigging were both in the way, but outside Bob confirmed that they were weaving a little, like a Barry Sanders touchdown run.

"We haven't got that autopilot trained yet. If you've got a book on training autopilots, please send it over when we pass reading materials."

"Well, we're ready whenever you are."

"OK, let's get started."

"Fust, we want you to idle back, then put her in neutral and let the ole gal come to a stop, and then just stay there. Joe will do the maneuvering. He will come up bow to bow and slip up beside you on starboard. When we get the two forepeaks opposite each other I'll come out and toss the mouse with a light line attached to one of your boys. That light line will be attached to a heavier line that will have a fish basket on it. Haul that in and trade contents, then we'll take it back. Make sure you keep the line tight both going and coming, or you'll have a load of wet books. Yer forepeak is about six and a half feet above the water line, so that's the room you have to play with. Just keep the line tight, no slack in it."

"Gotcha, Dave."

"Just remember you don't do anything over there. Joe will do the maneuvering from the *I.* .It gets too complicated if both boats are trying to get position on one another and neither one knows what the other has in mind."

"OK."

"Joe's going to come up on your starboard side about fifteen or twenty feet away. Get a couple of the boys on the forepeak to catch the mouse and haul the line in.

The other boys can round up the things coming over here."

Joe came up a scant twenty feet away. It looked to the boys like they could step across. Fortunately, no one tried it.

Bob sent the boys to get things set up as Dave suggested. Joe pulled up, bow to bow, just a little off line to starboard. The sea was like glass, with swells less than a foot high. The mouse was a bolt wrapped with tape, and attached to the light line, then to the transfer line, and finally to the fish basket. Rick and Dan were given the job of retrieving the transfer lines, primarily because they had been football quarterbacks in high school, and both had played baseball as well. After the catch was made, Joe hooked the Beckett straps over the wheel spokes, and slowly backed off until the two boats were separated by about twenty yards. The forepeak rises about six feet above the waterline. So the trick was to keep the transfer line tight during the operation, preventing seawater from corrupting the magazines and books.

Dan was fidgety. Bob suspected he wanted to get started on his fish, so Bob came out to the foredeck, and told Dan," Go ahead, get your guys going and I'll finish up with Rick on closing down this transfer operation."

Dan had secured some 2 X 6 short lengths that had been used as blocking to secure some of the below decks cargo, so Dan, Walt, and Jimmy started in on the horde of fish on the aft deck. No official count was taken but Dan later said there must have been fifty or so. They de-finned them, headed and gutted them, and scaled them. Dan gathered his finished beauties in a bucket and retired into the galley where he got the Crisco, cornmeal, and flour out, waiting for the plaintive, "I'm hungry, when are gonna eat?" (Some things are so inbred in youth that it would take two men, a little boy, and an act of Congress to change!)

The first load came over with no problems, as did ensuing loads. The transfer equipment went back aboard *Alpha I.* The thirty-minute exercise was over, and they could continue on their way.

In the late afternoon, Dave came up on the VHF saying to anyone within earshot, "Look to the south. There's a long ship out there. It looks to me like a supertanker. It's hull down, but in the binocs, I can see both houses, fore and aft, and they are a looooong way apart. My guess is that it's a supertanker. Who's on the horn?"

Walt replied, "I am, Cap'n Dave."

"Do you see that ship?"

"Yes, sir."

"How far away would you say it is?"

"I don't know. Maybe four or five miles. That's just a guess."

"That's about right. That's what I would say, as well. If so, we'll get the wake from it in about thirty minutes. Check your time."

Twenty-seven minutes later, the *Alpha II* started a gentle roll.

Walt explained to Jimmy, "Dave spotted a supertanker passing us, and was just calling it to our attention."

The boys were still gathered around the wheelhouse when one of them exclaimed, "What is that!"

chapter fourteen

STORM NO.2

Sperm, Orca Whales

"What is what?"

"That! It looks like a mini-waterspout."

Almost immediately, Dave was back on the horn. "Walt, you still there?"

"Yessir."

"Well, look toward us. You will see some sperm whales. Looks like we're in a pod of them."

"Yes, we saw them. I was just going back to to get the rest and let them see them as well."

"OK, but let me know when you get everyone together because them sperms are sure interesting animals."

"OK, Captain Dave, will do."

Walt rounded up the crew, now dispersed after the supertanker steamed out of sight. He got them all forward, both on the forepeak and in the wheelhouse. The wheelhouse windows were open, that is, they had been lowered into the well below the windows to allow the slight breeze from their forward progress to provide as much cooling as possible. So those gathered on the forepeak were privy to what was said over the VHF.

In the meantime, Bob came up, having been awakened from his snooze by the VHF traffic, and asked Walt, "What was all that? "Walt filled him in. Bob was intrigued and went out to look for himself. The boys told him the whale they saw must have been forty to fifty feet long, for it was traveling the same way as the boat and seemed to overlap the length of the *II.* No one disputed their reasoning nor the apparent discrepancy in the boat's length.

Walt got Dave back, telling him that all hands (and feet) were on deck. Dave began his story on the sperm whale, "There was this man named 'Pegleg Nye', a whaler from back east somewhere. They had caught two whales, and had a third one beside their longboat. Pegleg hit the whale with an explosive harpoon to kill it, and the whale reacted by thrashing its tail around and knocking Pegleg overboard. His leg wound up in the whale's mouth clamped tightly between the whale's teeth and its upper jaw. Then the whale sounded. You know, sperms have been known to dive more than 10,000 feet down. They are bottom feeders and normal feeding range is about 3,000 feet, feeding primarily on squid and octopus. It's called a toothed animal because their lower jaw has teeth about 7 inches long with wide spaces between them, and with the jaw closed these teeth fit into sockets in the upper jaw. But, fortunately for Pegleg, the beast died by the explosive harpoon charge, and bobbed back to the surface. His crew freed Pegleg, and he was known as Jonah until he died of natural causes at the age of 79. Sometimes, if they become irritated, a sperm will sound, and then come up under the boat and smashing the wooden hull with its twenty-ton head, leaving the whalers to find other transportation back to their mother ship."

That was not a particularly comforting thought to leave with those on board the *Alpha II*, what with six or seven of those monsters in that pod cruising around them. And monsters they were. The mature sperm whale will tip the scales at 50 to 60 tons, with a battering ram head twenty feet long or so. If you cut the head off a sperm whale, there aren't many living rooms in the country that would be able to fit that much head inside! There are other gargantuan details of the sperm whale that would discourage any right-minded individual from picking a fight with one. In fact, the boys learned a healthy respect for those whalers of yesteryear who put their lives on the line for the wax-like ambergris the sperm whale produces.

But Bob was preoccupied with the weather – or rather the lack of definition of the weather. Call it an omen, a premonition, but he was busy twisting dials trying to locate a weather frequency. He finally picked up an English broadcast out of Monrovia or Cape Ann reporting marine weather with a weather disturbance centered about 500 miles SSW of the *Alpha's* present position – or rather what he believed the *Alpha's* present position to be. With no sun shot for over a day now, they couldn't be sure. It was classified as a tropical depression and was expected to strengthen over the next 48 hours. There was minimal apparent danger involved because they were headed more or less away from the affected area.

Discretion being the better part of valor, Bob thought it wise to alert Joe. "*Alpha I, Alpha II.* Come back."

Dave answered, "Yeah, Bob, what's up?"

"Actually, I need Joe, or better that I have the both of you. Is Joe around?"

"Yeah, he's still up and about. He's coming."

"Yes, Bob, I'm on."

"Gentlemen, I just picked up a marine weather broadcast out of either Monrovia or Cape Ann that said there is a tropical depression, as near as I can figure it, about 500 miles SSW of our position, and it's expected to strengthen over the next 48 hours. Just a heads up"

"OK. Thanks. You say you got that from Monrovia or Cape Ann?"

"Yes, the station's ID faded in and out, but the storm's lat/longs came in pretty strong. If you can get a two-way hookup with any weather reporting station out this way, I'd be very happy if you kept us in the loop. Figuring from my last plot, we should be about 1200 miles off the coast of Africa. That should get us there in three to four days, don't you think?"

"Yes, unless we hit another storm out here. We'll keep you in the loop if there's one raised out here."

"OK, we'll keep you plugged in."

Finally, Walt said, "When are we gonna eat?"

Dan heard that exchange, and recruiting help from Jimmy, dashed to the galley with Jimmy following. Most of the preparatory work had been done while the reading materials transfer was winding down and the deck was sluiced off.

What Dan put on the table was more than adequate. It consisted of a powdered egg omelette with flying fish and oven baked toast. Dan's donuts were exonerated. The crew was to look for other avenues to vilify Dan's pride. Dan clearly had won that one.

Late in the afternoon the rain started. Bob figured he would take advantage of the opportunity for a shower. He filled a bucket of tap water from the lazarette to rinse with, stripped, and headed out onto the aft deck. (What he wasn't aware of and what the boys didn't tell him until the trip was over and their cameras stowed was that they were busy recording this whole episode with their cameras from the relative safety of the hatch in the crew's quarters and the one in the head.) After soaping up, he rinsed off with the lazarette water to establish at least the sense of a fresh-water shower. After toweling down, he said he felt four pounds lighter and at least that much better. The rain was steady, not wind blown at the moment, and each of the boys enjoyed a shower as well, as did Joe and Dave and the Ghanaians on the *Alpha I*.

After their showers, Bob had them stow all loose items on deck and run lifelines from the wheelhouse down both sides and around the corners of the deckhouse, and secure them on the port side, to the winch mounts, and on the starboard from the wheelhouse to the galley/crew house hatch, and then another line from there to the engine room hatch. Walt was given strict instruction not to go anywhere near the lifelines in the event of contrary seas without waking Bob first, so they had an alert on his wanderings. However, it was Walt's luck to have drawn the midnight to six A.M. stint, and he insisted on pulling his shift. The other thing they did was to lower the outriggers to lower the ship's center of gravity, improving stability.

It seemed like overkill, for the first part of the evening the wind freshened a little, but they were driving into an area of confused seas – one body of water, say an off shore flow, is opposite to that generated by wind or other external sources, creating a conflict between the two opposing generators – hence the confusion regarding the height, direction, frequency, and the severity of the generated waves was random and unpredictable.

The winds continued to increase after Bob sacked out. He figured he might have much to do in the morning so he'd get a little sleep while he could. Then just after midnight, it happened. The boat pitched violently upward tossing Bob up and out of his bunk almost instantly. Another wave crashed into the right side of the ship moving eighty tons of ship an estimated twelve inches sideways to port. The bunk Bob was sleeping on had six-inch side boards to prevent dumping its occupant on the deck in such circumstances. When *Alpha II* quit its gyrations and gravity held rule, it left Bob suspended immediately over the side rail, and then let him go. A very sharp pain struck Bob between the shoulder blades for a moment. The pain was excruciating. He figured the worst - that his back was broken. But as he lay there, he found that he could move his arms and legs, and that in time the pain was lessening. It was painful just rolling over or rising, but the pitching of the boat indicated that this was more severe a storm than the squall line they had encountered north of Cuba. And since Bob could not get back to sleep, he felt he was far more useful on deck. As he put his feet on the deck, it was a shock of the wake up variety like walking through a wading pool back home or like stepping into an ankle-deep hole full of water that was totally unexpected – comparatively cold and in the dark of night. It created imaginary sensations of more severe consequences.

Walt had his hands full. Green water was coming over the bow, and pouring through both the port and starboard the hatches, which were cracked a bit to allow the lifelines to be tied off, and around the forward glass areas. Water was everywhere, everywhere it should not have been!

Bob struggled against the pitch of the boat to the wheelhouse deck, and wondered about the safety of the boys. Walt took one look at Bob, and asked him, "Dad, are you all right?" His face had lost its color, to where Bob appeared to Walt as one of Disney's sheet clad characters in the cartoon shorts featuring Chester, the ghost. Bob had all the trappings of a featured cartoon, except the humor.
Bob's answer was barely discernable, "No, I think I'm all right. One of those waves tossed me up and apparently another caught the boat and moved the bunk out from under me. When I came down, I landed on the sideboard. I guess nothing is broken, but a few minutes ago I would not have bet on that!"

There was no means of communication between the helm and the crews' quarters, the only means being to venture a trip to visually check on the others. At that time, no one felt the urge to make that trip.

Bob switched on the searchlight but it was no help. Every so often, he imagined he could see the lights of *Alpha I*, but they would disappear, not to reappear, no matter how long he stared into the blackness. Bob guessed the seas were about fifteen feet or more judging from the view out of the wheelhouse. The wheelhouse deck was six feet above the waterline and the wheelhouse was about seven feet tall. Those incoming waves would often dwarf the wheelhouse, and just as often overrun it.[-] it was hard to distinguish what was wave and what were the effects of the bow dipping into Davey Jones' locker. The weep holes in the cabins could hardly handle the flow of water. Fortunately, the scuppers at the rails allowed the bulk of those torrents a means of escape. The ship would ride up over the crest of a wave, then dive off into the ensuing trough, burying the bow into the green water. In an instant, the world, as much of it as could be seen, took on an eerie cast, a greenish glow, as though you were wearing dark green glasses but seeing the boiling, turbulent green at the height of tornados in the Midwest.

The feeling of helplessness abounded. All aboard understood the meaning of "praying in earnest." When the ship took on one of those "dark green demons", it didn't matter what direction a person looked, even upward, it was all green. You didn't really know if you were upright, or were topsy turvy.

Then Rick came forward along the starboard lifeline.

The VHF came to life. "*Alpha II, Alpha I.* Come in."

Bob, being closest to the mike, answered, "Hi, we're still with you, if that's what you're interested in."

"That's a good start. No, I just wanted to bring you up to speed on this weather. Our current course and speed should have us clear of this by sometime in the afternoon. The storm is moving away to the west/northwest at about ten knots and we're going east about the same speed. That should give us a separation speed relative to the storm of about twenty knots, but the heaviest winds will be on the east side of the storm. So they will probably be with us for several days. This storm appears to differ from the one we faced going in to San Juan, where that one packed straight line winds. This is a more conventional rotational type with tropical storm or hurricane characteristics."

"Thanks, Joe. Thanks for the analysis. No one's been below since things started rattling around over here, so we don't have any idea what we'll find there. For a while it looked like Desco should have provided a periscope with this rig."

"Yes, I'll buy that. For a while we thought the same thing, but it isn't over yet. Just hang in there for another five or six hours and it should start getting better."

"OK, Joe. We'll give you a shout if we find anything out of the ordinary when we start moving around over here. Say, where are you?"

"I don't know where we are in relation to you, but I feel we're within a mile or two of each other. We were both subject to the same weather, currents, and winds, so if you were able to keep a reasonable harness on your heading, that's where I figure we should both be. *Alpha I* out."

The boat shuddered and shook, a not-so-gentle reminder that they were not clear of anything just yet.

Dan came forward to announce that coffee was made, but they had to go back to the galley to get a cup. He didn't want to try toting several cups of hot coffee over an uncooperative deck. He had problems in with making the coffee.

Walt crawled up from the captain's cabin where he was trying to get a weather station in Monrovia or elsewhere. Bob envisioned a catastrophe there, remembering Walt's inability to handle the rigors of a fairly easy ride into San Juan. "Walt, how did you leave my cabin?"

"I made no contributions to the cause – any cause – front door or back."

"Actually, I came up on my hands and knees if you must know, Dad. I am ready for anything, whatever the cost." He didn't expand on the comment, so everyone was left to their own interpretation. Bob chose not to have him elaborate.

The storm seemed to be abating a little, but the next wave belied that thought bringing more green water over the bow, inundating the wheelhouse and Bob's cabin again. When one of those massive waves climbed over the forepeak and covered the wheelhouse it was as if the lights went out and the whole world took on a green ethereal glow. But in seconds (which at times seemed to stretch into hours) it would clear up, leaving the crew to look for the next one. One after another, that seemed to be the marching orders of the day. Perhaps it was just the thought that they were adjusting to the sensations created when a wave washed over the boat, but the crew seemed now to take the shudders and creaking in stride, all the while fearing something more devastating. Even though the storm was more severe in some ways to their previous encounter, it seemed they had a better handle on combating its wiles. Perhaps that was because of their baptism of fire in the squall line. Confidence is a good trait unless it is overused or not placed into proper perspective.

The thought of coffee just twenty feet away finally got the best of Walt and he braved the blustery wind. For bravery, though, Jimmy took the prize. Staggering along the lifeline to the engine room hatch, he descended down the handrail to check the bilges, which had water now up to the deck planking covering the drive shaft tunnel. He started the bilge pumps, and waited long enough to be assured they were operating and no problems were apparent, then headed up out of those narrow confines. Walt, working the lifeline along because the combination of wind and sea on the boat still did not make for good footing, met Jimmy coming forward, curious as to what was happening and what had happened in the galley. Dan had mastered the winds and seas just a pot of coffee earlier, and was eager to sit for a while. So the three of them met at the galley doorway and decided to all break for coffee.

Bob also thought a cup of coffee sounded very good, and he padded barefoot to the galley, leaving Rick at the helm. Jimmy and Walt were there discussing the storm, and Joe's prediction of when it might end. Five or six hours was not particularly encouraging news, but it was better than what they had envisioned. It was something to look forward to!

Their coffee was getting better all the time. Bob felt that by the time they reached Tema it would be safe to offer it to others. Right now, it still could not be considered a peace offering. But when the noon hour passed, Bob decided they should look below and see what damage they had suffered, so he recruited Walt and Jimmy to go below with him and start the bilge pumps. Jimmy interrupted him, "Capt'n Bob, excuse me, but the bilge pumps are already on."

"Oh, when did that happen?"

"As soon as I felt that the boat was stable enough, I went below to see if we suffered any damage. I couldn't see any, but I did kick the bilge pumps on since we did have a lot of water in the bilges. It was up over the drive shaft tunnel."

"Well why don't you go back down and cut the pumps off if the bilge water is down, then look over the fuel tanks for leakage because the ship has taken a pretty severe beating. And Jimmy, that was good thinking. You took all the precautions we had talked about en route to San Juan. But I have one bone to pick with you. In seas like we had, do not go anywhere without telling someone where you are going and for about how long, especially a place like the engine room. There's enough machinery down there just aching to get its hands on you and it could be hours before you'd be missed. The same goes for a stroll on deck in moderate or heavy seas. But thanks anyway, for doing what you saw needed to be done. I'm just happy we don't have to call your parents in a difficult situation. Speaking of the deck, when we get clear of this storm we want to check the deck load to make sure it is secure after the pounding it took."

By late afternoon the winds had died down and the seas moderated. Joe was right. It appeared they could return to the normal crossing routine, except they had not had a sun shot since the day before yesterday at noon. Bob tried to get radio fixes on Abidjan and another station on the west coast of Africa, but the signals were not strong enough to give an accurate fix on the station. So, they just kept on chugging. The skies were still overcast, and promised to remain that way for the next several days, which was not a problem at the moment.

Dan then put on his chef's hat, which he had fashioned out of an old paper grocery bag from San Juan, and he took steaks out for the second time on this leg of the trip to celebrate the weathering of the storm. That left them with one round of steaks, which were to be consumed after they sighted land, African land. So, they feasted sumptuously that evening, but with no land in sight.

The cloud deck lifted a little and improving visibility, but still obscuring the sky. About two miles off the starboard stern, they visually picked up *Alpha I*. Rick called to tell those in the other boat that he had a visual on them. Dave answered, "Where have you been? We've had you in our sight for twenty minutes already."

"We had every teacup over here in use and weren't able to bail fast enough to stay ahead of this water."

"What happened to your bilge pumps?"

"We've been trolling for mermaids for you. So when we mentioned it, we said she was for Captain David Banks and the best offer we got was to hook you up with someone's grandmother! We do have a radio patch if you want it."

"Naw, I'll leave her for the next fellow. Thanks anyway."

The next morning, Walt and Jimmy had duty, and one of them spotted several orcas, or killer whales, nearby. There were at least twenty in this pod. Bob was half dozing, half awake when this whale talk got through to him. Walt said, "Let's find out what Dave knows about these things. "*Alpha I, Alpha II.* Dave, you there?"

"Who is this, Walt? This is Joe. Dave is still sacked out. Wait a minute, I hear him rustling the sheets down there, so I expect he'll be up here in a minute. OK. Here he is."

"Hi, Dave. We appreciated the rundown you gave us on the sperm whale. We're now running in a bunch of killer whales. Do you know how they got their name? Is it a man eater?"

Jimmy whispered to Walt that he was going to see who all was awake, feeling another interesting lecture was about to begin. They were all awake, and when the word "killer whales" was mentioned, their sleep became a thing of history.

Dave continued, "No, it's not known as a man eater, but keep in mind that anything that big, and with all the tools that this one has, is bound to be dangerous. Its moniker is probably based on the fact that it will eat almost anything that swims, including fish, octopus, squid, even young blue whales, sharks, and birds. They are a little faster than the sperm by about ten percent capable of about 30 miles per hour. They hunt in groups, teaming up with others of the same pod to overpower larger prey. They are of the toothed variety, although not as large in any dimension as the sperm or the great blue. They have teeth in both the upper and lower jaws. Their life expectancy is about 60 years for the male and 90 years for the female. Orcas are the largest member of the dolphin family, and talk about eat! These beasts will eat around 550 pounds of their catch a day. But that can't compare with 1000 pounds for the sperm's diet. I love squid, but it seems like you get a couple of good-sized pods of these things around, there wouldn't be much left for us humans, would there?"

The orcas moved with the two boats for four hours, then disappeared. The boys wondered whether they had run across squid, fish, or some other orca delicacy. Jimmy and Dan figured they had a good chance of catching some of those delicacies, provided they had enough line to get down to the orca's feeding depth. Dave said orcas didn't hunt much below 100 feet, much less than the 3,000 feet ascribed to the sperm whale. But, since Jimmy and Dan didn't have much to do except for Dan's putting chow on the table that night, they felt this would be as good as anything else they could think of to become gainfully involved in that day. They rigged the diving planes for maximum depth, which at that setting considering the angle of entrance into the water of the line and 300 feet of line should run about the depth they were looking for. Their bait was flying fish they had caught just the day before.

It was hard to realize that so much had happened in just one day.

Bob and Rick were spending their time wisely, studying more about the sea. But one thought kept coming back to haunt Bob, *Why did we have such poor signal strength when we tried to reach Abidjan? That should have come in strong because we should have been 100 to 200 miles out.* He went up and flicked the Furuno on. It registered over 5000 feet depth, so maybe the storm changed some things. *Oh well,* he reasoned, *maybe we will get a sun shot tomorrow.* He went back up and called, "*Alpha I ,Alpha I, Alpha II.* Come back."

"Bob, how are you guys doing over there?" It was Dave. Joe had **[h-d]** a lousy night and was sleeping it off.

"It doesn't look like we suffered any hurt, but I've been bothered by one thing. When we ran into that storm, I was trying to get Abidjan for a weather update. I could not get any strength in my signal, not enough to get a fix on the station. Of course this is not a good radio for weather reception – I think it's made by the same people that make the Mickey Mouse watch. Just now, I went up and turned on the Furuno and we're into waters now that are far deeper than we're supposed to be according to the charts. I just hope we can get a shot tomorrow. Has Joe said anything about when this overcast is going to clear up?"

"No, I think Joe figures we're all in the same boat. I know he's looking for a sun shot just like the rest of us."

"Boy, what I wouldn't give for an Omega navigation unit about now. You can get the cheap ones for about $2,500. When you guys get to fishing over here something like that would be invaluable for locating productive areas and getting you back to them. Even the cheap units will locate you to within four miles**. [a-d]** That's close enough for government work!"

"Dave, when you set up shop over here, why don't you propose equipping these boats with a more efficient navigation system? It doesn't have to be something we forgot, technology is changing all the time. You would just be keeping pace with the changing times. Talk to Joe about that, and check out the equipment available."

They ran into some scattered showers, but they still had the winds **now** from **the North**, **which** had moderated substantially. They did not run into any noontime sunshine, however.

They endured another day like that. In fact, it was getting boring just to drive ahead, check systems, check oil, check bilges. That would occupy one of the men on board, but what of the rest? One other would be at the helm. That still left three to devise mischief.

chapter fifteen

THE DISAGREEMENT

Bob had his own problems. He was still brooding over the fact that they cold not raise Abidjan then, and still couldn't. It didn't make sense to him. So he decided they should move up to the 100-fathom line and maybe get a visual on major landmarks to pinpoint their progress. After all, this would be the third day without a position report! *I've got to get hold of Joe and get closer to shore, get a handle on our location.*

"*Alpha I, Alpha II.* Come back."

Joe was on. "Yes, Bob, what's up?"

"Joe, we're driving right toward Nigerian waters, which we don't want to get into. The Nigerians have just acquired two German patrol boats, basically to keep interlopers out of their waters. And I think I heard that they widened their coastal water to twelve miles. This is the third day since we've had a sun shot position, right?"

"The patrol boats I heard about, but the coastal waters I had not. But it's possible."

"They didn't get those patrol boats just to be spending money. I think we'll find them out searching for some itinerant vessels to make their payroll this month. Remember the Mayaguez in Puerto Rico? That's almost exactly like the North Koreans pulled on us, and it took the US about a year to get that cleared."

"Bob, what are you saying?"

"I'm suggesting it would make sense to move up to the 100-fathom line and maybe get some visual landmarks to establish our position before we get into Nigerian waters."

"I think we're a little early for that yet. By my dead reckoning, we've got several days yet until we hit, or even come close to, Nigerian waters."

"OK Joe, I'll go along with that, but only for a limited time. One more day. At noon tomorrow, if we don't have a sun shot by then, we're going north to the 100-fathom line."

The next day dawned overcast, with scattered showers so the plan to head north was moved to the front burner. Joe still didn't agree. But Bob stood his ground, and said, "At noon *Alpha II* is going north. I can't twist your wheel from over here, but I would really appreciate your coming along."

"We'll see."

The weather had not changed by noon, so the *Alpha II* took up a north heading, leaving *Alpha I* plowing on eastward.

"*Alpha I, Alpha II.* Come back."

"Yes, Bob, we see you have turned north, so you're going ahead with your plan."

"It's the only sure way I can see out of this pile of doggie doo we're in. We'll be listening on Channel 16. *Alpha II* out."

Meanwhile, on board the *Alpha I* what was destined to become a heated discussion as just warming up.

Dave said, "Joe, how long have you had your master's papers, twenty years?"

"Oh, it's probably more than that. Let's see, I got them before that oceanographic stint, a year before, so that would make it in the early fifties."

"So you've got to be concerned about this trip, right?"

"No, not really. Why, do you think I should be?"

"Yes, I do. If it was me sittin' here tryin' to figure out what's happenin', I'd be real concerned about my future."

"How so?"

"Well, we're trollin' along straight into an area that is patrolled by new Nigerian, call them gunboats, with no idea of where we are, and the Nigerian attitude is – or should be – to commandeer any vessel that violates our territorial waters without proper authorization. Why do people expand those territorial waters? Remember the Mayaguez in San Juan? They were caught in expanded territorial waters. The captain, in fact the whole crew, testified that they were clear of North Korean waters, but that didn't stop the North Koreans from claiming that was not true. It resulted in an international incident – one right now the U.S. does not need, not following so closely on the Mayaguez incident. And how will the board look at the ability of a ship's master who disregards a relatively safe way to determine position in favor of what? A potentially misguided feeling that dead reckoning navigation takes on more legitimacy than visual landmarks?"

"All right, point taken. I'll think 'bout it."

"OK, Joe, you're the boss. I just hope we don't run into any trouble this close to the end of the trip. I personally don't look forward to a year or so on a Nigerian jail diet."

"That's something to be considered."

On *Alpha II*, as time went by, premonitions of doom danced in Bob's mind fed by the quietness of the ship. Funny, it never occurred to him before that the ship was ever this quiet. Now, every time a little static emitted from the VHF, Bob's ears perked up. Two hours, nothing. Four hours, still nothing. He went to his bunk, just to think. *Was he confusing something? Was he becoming paranoid?* That was a mistake, for he thought of nothing constructive, nothing that would appease those waiting in anticipation at Tema. There would be the usual legal hassles and, worst of all, Bob would be in the middle of it. Then there was Charley and the Bank, and Bob and his boys would be half a world from home. But Jo should be in Ghana by the time they docked....maybe even now! And Shirley Temple Black was the U.S. ambassador. He might even get to meet her. No, the price was too great.

Why doesn't Joe swallow his pride, if that's what holds him back, and call? Why doesn't that bloody thing come to life? Oh well, people, you can't understand them, that's why there are psychiatrists, I guess. Then he remembered that Charley graduated in dual fields: psychiatry and business administration. He had to be dealt with as well! How long has it been since we turned north? A check of his watch indicated it had been over six hours.

A little later Jimmy shouted down to him, "Mr. Murray, we've got something on the radio! It's scratchy, but maybe you can make something of it!"

Bob bounded up the steps into the wheelhouse, his back still objecting to the exertion, listening intently for Joe or Dave. All he heard was a little chatter between vessels arriving. *Arriving?* Arriving *where?* The continuing chatter confirmed these hidden vessels were inbound to Lagos, a place where Bob did not want to be. So he changed course to 315 degrees.

Mere minutes later, Bob heard a familiar scratching sound from the VHF. He thought he heard, "*Alpha II*". He grabbed the mike like a drowning man might grab a life preserver and called back, "*Alpha I,* did you call?"

There was more scratching, more static, but nothing decipherable that he could take to the bank. But, there it was again. This time readable. "*Alpha II, Alpha I,* do you read?"

Bob was only too happy to tell them, "Roger – we read you four by five!"

"How far up are you?"

"We really can't tell yet, but we're showing about 260 fathoms and we're getting a lot of inbound radio traffic to Lagos on the VHF. Suggest you alter course to 315 degrees for at least an hour. Copy?"

"Roger. Going to 315 degrees, one hour plus, A*lpha I* .Out."

It had been eleven hours since they turned north, but Bob had no way of knowing where Joe was when he made the change. Bob did not want to give out information the Nigerians could use to locate them and thought they were bound to be listening. The Furuno read out 260 fathoms. *Getting closer*, thought Bob. Also on the positive side, the seas had moderated, now with only six to eight foot swells even though they were driving into an area close to shore where the depth would begin to affect the wave action. Depending on the slope of the bottom, they should make the line in about another hour. Walt and Jimmy were on duty, and the others were sacked out. After all, the clock had wound around them big time. It was six A.M. locally, but midnight in Clearwater/Largo. Bob decided to get a cup of coffee, so he padded barefoot back to the galley to see if Dan had left any coffee for the night shift. Yes, there was coffee, and Bob's faith having been restored, he recalled Dave's words about what makes these ships go – caffeine and diesel, in approximately equal amounts. Walt called to Bob that they were coming up on the 100-fathom line. Bob called back, "Bring it around 270 degrees, and cut the turns back to 1000. I'll be up in a minute to call Joe or Dave."

"Yes, Sir."

It was a pleasure working with someone who recognized and acknowledged authority, whether it be through upbringing or by fear of reprisal.

Bob, returning to the wheelhouse, called Joe or Dave - he didn't care which it was, "*Alpha I, Alpha II.* Come back."

Dave answered, "Yeah, Bob. What's up?"

"We're at the line waiting for you. When you get to the line, give us a shout and we'll try to hook up. Our power is cut back, heading at 270 degrees. Just sitting here, having a cup of coffee in your honor."

Dave said, "We *are* honored."

"You should be."

The coastline was in plain view now in the morning sun. The overcast skies appeared to be behind them. This day was to have the promise of a beautiful day. Perhaps it would prove to be the last one before home cooking, family, and friends.

Bob was lost again in thought, but the VHF brought him abruptly back to the present. Joe was on the radio asking, "This coastline you're looking at, what do you see? We're at the line, but there's no *Alpha II* here."

"Just a minute, Joe. I'll get the binocs. Well, there's a village with a small church in the middle of it. Out to the west there's just a row of palm trees along the coastline. But to the east, it looks like there is a city there and that there are suburbs to it. This little village may be a suburb. That city may be Cotanou."

Joe asked a few more questions and said, "Give me a few minutes to look up those landmarks in the *Coastal Pilot*."

"OK."

Joe came back in less than five minutes, saying, "Bob, I can't be sure, for so many of these coastal villages look the same with a church and all, but I'm pretty sure we're west of you. We're going to turn her about and go east for an hour. If we have made no contact with you by then, I may ask you to get a better look at that city. Besides, we should get a sun shot at noon today. That won't help a lot because then we'll know where we are, but it won't tell us where you are."

"It makes sense that you are west of us because there are not many cities along this stretch of coast. The only two I see are Lagos and Cotanou. I don't think we are east of Lagos, so I'll head westbound and hopefully meet you halfway."

The two ships squared off about ten miles apart and commenced a maritime "chicken" game on the high seas. There were ten pairs of eyes on *Alpha II* and twelve pairs on *Alpha I* scanning, no searching, the horizon for each other. There were many false alarms, mainly on account of the many fishing canoes plying the inshore waters. Most of these were much closer to shore then 100 fathoms (600 feet), a depth well beyond the cast nets' effective depth used by these fishermen who would fish from within 10 to 30 feet of water. But the eye plays serious tricks on open water. It makes distances very difficult to gauge, as Bob remembered from their experience in sighting the whales. So the boys would call out, "Here they come," or "I see them," only to be tricked by their own eyesight But when *Alpha I* did appear over the horizon, there was no mistaking it. Its outriggers were down and it was pushing a load of water. It did not resemble any of the canoes seen along that coast.

Cheers erupted from the decks of *Alpha II*, and the VHF sprang to life. Joe was still on. "Bob, we've got an eye on you, and I want to apologize. I was dead wrong in continuing east back there. I know now that would have put us in the middle of Lagos harbor or worse. Thanks for saving our cajones." So Joe did know a little Spanish after all.

"We're all here now with no excess baggage hanging 'round waiting to ask embarrassing questions. So as they say, 'All's well that ends well'. Let's get our belly full of fish and get these floating hotels with no maid service into port and docked."

GETTING NEAR THE END : We're beginning to smell good cookin'.

"Bob, we want to check the bottom between say, fifteen and twenty fathoms. You won't have nets down, so I suggest you take off on the 20-fathom line and we'll sneak in and pick up the 15-fathom line. We'll have our try net down, so if we run into anything we'll break off and come around for another run at it with the mains out. If we do, just kick her out of gear and wait for us to get lined up again."

Alpha II took off to look for the 20-fathom line with Joe and Dave right behind just off to starboard heading for fifteen fathoms.

Dave was running the aft deck of the *Alpha I*, so he let his try net down. (The try net is a small version of the main net and is used to check the catch or to confirm that the ship is in good fish, shrimp, or whatever. It is about 4 x 6 feet, much smaller than the main and much easier to handle. Usually on its own winch, it can be handled independently of the main net which is generally a balloon type.) About twenty minutes into the sample, Dave picked up several hits on the try net, and pulled it in to check. It showed several fish and some tiger shrimp - large ones, almost like stunted lobster. Joe heeled the *I* around and retraced his steps back about a half mile, then came forward again, with the big nets fully deployed.

Alpha II's VHF came to life again. Joe said," Fellas, I think we'll play around here for a while. Seems some of these fish and shrimp were just waiting for us, and we wouldn't want to disappoint them now, would we?"

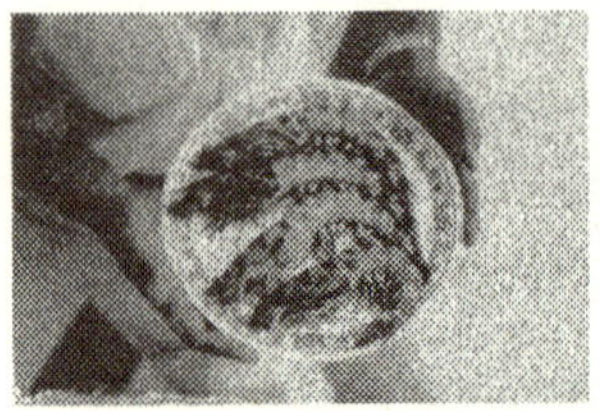

A SAMPLING OF THE HARVEST INBOUND TO TEMA

They brought the nets in and by fishermen's rationale, it wasn't much of a haul, but you could not prove that by the reaction of the Ghanaians. They dove in to clear the nets with more gusto than had been seen by Joe or Dave – or for that matter by Rick for as long as he sailed with them! They were like kids at Halloween – their candy bucket ran over. Bob pulled off to the side and let Joe and Dave have the stage.

They had two more good passes, landing both fish and shrimp in each pass. And the shrimp! These ranged from about 6 to 12 count. That's the number of shrimp it takes to make a pound! Joe and Dave both figured they had enough aboard indeed for dog and pony show time, so they opted to bring this exercise to a close. Bob agreed as well. The nets were retrieved, loose gear was stowed, and the two boats headed west again - this time looking for solid terra firma, and to a world that recognized directions as right and left, not starboard and port. Bob and the boys were ready for the change back to what used to be normal. In short, Bob and the boys had had it. They were ready for this adventure to draw to a close. Perhaps that is not the way to put it. They were more ready for the next adventure to begin! They had had a good educational time. But, as one of them had said, "Enough is enough!" But would they do it again? They answered in chorus, "You bet! When do we leave?"

It was late afternoon when they entered the breakwater at Tema, pulled up to the dock by now pretty full with fishing craft. So after talking to the dock master, they learned Charley had been at the dock earlier in the afternoon and would return about nine A.M. The group felt one more night aboard would not hurt them. So both boats stopped, minus the Ghanaians who had left saying, "Not to worry, we will find our way home, and be back next day." There were handshakes and back slapping as the Ghanaians cleared customs and re-entered their homeland.

The Alpha boats retreated a mile off shore to remain clear of inbound shipping traffic and set their mast lights with their minds zeroed in on a normal life again, planning their trip home and catching up with a month on the road, or sea as the case may be. Catching up meant first contacting Bobi (or (Debi) letting her know they had made it, and what their plans were for completing the trip. Jo should be en route to Ghana with Sandi. Or, they may already be in Ghana. They would find out tomorrow. Setting a watch through the night proved to be more a nuisance than a problem, for the boys were so fired up that that little thought was given to sleep. Many what if scenarios were explored that night, so by morning he boys had a pretty good idea what kind of hand the near future was to deal them, and what they could do with it.

The docking facilities at Tema consisted of an inner basin lying essentially north and south which handled smaller craft, its entrance along the southeast corner of the basin. Texaco had their fuelling facilities near the entrance, a fact that did not escape Dave Banks' ever-curious eye. On the west side of the basin was the cargo wharf, separating the heavy ocean-going freighters from other marine enterprise. The mix in the basin was composed mainly of tug boats, small fishing vessels, and some pleasure boats. Most of the latter types put in at Cotanou or Abijdjan because of the availability of upscale accommodations and the resplendent night-life.

Unknown to any of the neophyte sailors (nor to Joe and Dave as well) Charley had secured a small two bedroom rental property in Tema for Joe and Dave since they would be staying on to run the Alpha boats. The first order after docking was to offload the catch, then secure storage for the spares brought aboard *Alpha II*, and then unload the Buick station wagon and clear customs on it, something the Bank of Ghana was very helpful in accomplishing.

So when the boats docked in the morning, it was as if a new set of orders had been drawn up overnight, with Bob and the boys drawn into its vortex – a whirlpool with no end in sight. But as they docked, Walt broke the short leash he had been on since San Juan, all on account of a dock-side pineapple vendor. When *Alpha II* finally docked, the boys made a production out of it. They lined up at the rail, and one by one broad jumped onto the dock, landing flat footed amid screams of delight from Ghanaian youngsters on the docks. The boys kept their footing and moved ahead with a single purpose, to visit the pineapple vendor and sample some of her wares. Each of the boys and Bob opted for a pineapple apiece, except for

Walt. Walt picked out two big, healthy-looking specimens and a hand of bananas. He went to the galley and brought a large chef's knife to slice the pineapple, took all back to the aft rail where the rest had gathered with their plunder. The vendor had topped the pineapples. All that remained for the boys and Bob to do was to slice them into large sweet cartwheels – a job they attacked with gusto.

When the dust had settled, the boys had finished their single pineapples and Walt his two. Within the hour, however, Walt was feeling the effects of overindulgence. He was reacting with a major league case of diarrhea, brought on primarily by the diet they been on the past two or three weeks. The sudden, drastic change in diet did not bode well with his digestive system. Some of the other boys had mild cases of the same ailment. [B-t] What complicated the situation was the fact that there were only the two heads - one in each of the Alpha boats, and six, sometimes seven customers waiting for the facilities! Someone, noting their dilemma, pointed out a portable john on the dock, and mentioned the dock offices where the Dock Master's office was with additional facilities. This facility was the new "branch office" for the crew. A "four holer," it proved to be the salvation of the boys.

Alpha I put in at the fish unloading facility at the end of the docks, and Dave and Joe walked over to customs and immigration. Bob took the boys' passports into customs and immigration as well

At the deepwater end of the wharf, one of the Senagalese trawlers was docked. Joe was curious as to why he had misjudged his position so badly, so he headed for the trawler. Joe had navigated on the chart basis that prevailing currents were opposing them on the ocean at about 3 knots all the way from St. Augustine, verified many times by their sun shots. The distances traveled daily confirmed the opposing currents. But in discussions with the Senalgalese crew, the Senalgalese Omega plots showed currents in the Bight of Biafra reversed, flowing into the Bight making a net change to their actual speed relative to a fixed point, instead of about 7 knots eastbound – as much, roughly, as a 6-knot differential over what was plotted as 7 knots and what was realized as 13 knots. Joe figured that the currents had a problem of circulation in the wide entrance to the Bight. Even if he cut the effects in half to maybe 3 knots. Three knots for 40 hours would make a theoretical difference of 120 miles. That was his answer. Currents change, winds change. Seas change. He would remember this lesson. Fortunately, no one was hurt in this learning curve, which is not often the case. Joe was somewhat vindicated by the change in currents but not wholly absolved because the 100-fathom line would have offered a positive visual fix on their position. To Joe's credit,,he acknowledged this.

Alpha II had a dockside berth, but the harbormaster talked to Bob and suggested relocating the *II* to a new berth in the customs area where the station wagon and spares could be unloaded under the watchful eye of the customs officials. Later that day, *Alpha II* became a beehive of activity. The rigging that had been temporarily removed to load the station wagon was removed again to provide access to the vehicle. After off-loading the wagon, Dave moved the boat to the Texaco fuelling dock near the entrance to the basin. The weld repair to the Kohler exhaust and the damage to the wheelhouse on *Alpha I* was noted and reported.

Meanwhile the *Alpha I* was setting at the north end of the dock, and the catch off-loaded. All that remained to do on *Alpha I* was the cleaning of the hold, which the Ghanaian crew who had returned from their homes rather belatedly, were now setting out to accomplish. While this was being done, Joe took the opportunity to visit *Alpha II.*

Bob was in the wheelhouse reorganizing the papers from the trip, when Joe called out, "Bob are you in?"

"Yes, Joe, I'm up forward in the wheelhouse."

Joe surveyed the accommodations as the boys had left them on his way by the galley, and said, "You know, Bob, you're a lucky man! Compared to *Alpha I* the difference between these boats is as night and day! For example, the cookware the Ghanians used is still in the sink, with part of their last meal - or maybe it's the last two or three meals - in evidence."

"Dave and I talked about that last night. We agreed that we had to get these guys more conscious of their surroundings or there's bound to be someone getting hurt. And it won't be me. I think we've gotten their thinking on the right track. They all know by now that each is in this for the long haul, but we made them to understand that what benefits one benefits all. After they get the spares and stores offloaded from your ship they're to strip the bunks and wash the sheets and bedding. We'll make first class sailors out of them yet."

"That sounds good to me, but I'd like to check with the boys first and make sure they have all their personal items packed ready to go for home. When I was with Alaska Airlines, I was sent to Guinea to administer a technical assistance contract and was there two years. At that time, you were expected to employ native personnel for any job they could handle. So we had a cook, Souma; a houseboy, Salifoo, and a security, Diallo. All went well for a month. Then one day Diallo came to me, very proud, and gave me a portrait of himself he had had taken a few days earlier. It was an excellent likeness, perhaps too much so, for Diallo had on a dark suit, one of my ties, and my tie pin which stood out like a flashlight beacon in a dark alley! We were obligated by the local authorities to report any activity of that nature, so Diallo spent his next ten days in jail – and jail in the Republic of Guinea is anything but pleasant! After that experience he became an excellent guardian. But I don't want to offer anyone here the opportunity for an education on the same basis!"

Joe said, "I hear you. Let's see if the paperwork is all done on the wagon. If it is, then there's a lot that can be done with wheels. Say, Bob, how long will you be staying around?"

"I don't know. Probably a couple of days, perhaps up to a week. That will depend on Charley, and my wife and Sandi. You know, I don't even know what flight they are on. They could be in Accra right now. But first, I've got to find Charley. He'll have some answers to all our questions. And of course I'd like to get to see a little of Ghana while I'm here with Jo and the boys, especially Accra! We do have some friends here. They are missionaries and I have their address, so let's see if that car is ready to go, and what we will need to operate it in Ghana."

The two of them walked to where the station wagon was parked, and ran head-first into Charley and Peter Yeboah. Charley said, "Look there, Peter! That saves us a lot of time! Bob, Joe, we were just coming to get you. Jo is supposed to be in this afternoon. They were delayed in Dakar, but the last word from PanAm was that they're about two hours late. Peter is going to get the car out of hock for us and we'd better get to the airport. I've got accommodations arranged here in Tema for you and Dave, Joe. It's a small house – clean but plenty of room for the two of you. You will need an international drivers license, which Peter can help you with. Then you can drive back out here, and any supplies you still have on board can be loaded in the wagon and taken to the house. But come on, grab your stuff. We don't have much time until Jo and Sandi land!

Yeboah met them as he was coming out of customs and immigration, and joined the party. He said to them, "I've made arrangements for your entrance into Ghana, but each of you will have to appear at Immigrations with your passports to have visas issued and validated. Mr. Willis, the car is ready for you. I will take the captain and the other one here to the house that has been arranged for them. If there is anything more you gentlemen need, just call me. Here's my card."

Joe said, "There is nothing that a good hot shower won't take care of right now. Dave went over to Texaco to fuel the boats. I'll go find Dave and get the beans and stuff all lined up ready to go. And, Mr. Yeboah, please don't run an inspection, particularly on *Alpha I* until we get a chance to clean her insides out a bit."

Charley said, " I've arranged for the boys to go out day after tomorrow on PanAm's afternoon departure, connecting in New York to National Airlines into Tampa, but if Jimmy is going on to Tallahassee, I can have his travel extended to Tallahassee when I'm in there in Accra. Remind me when we get to town. That should give them enough time to cast their sea legs aside, and walk like homo sapiens again."

"Will do, Charley. I'm sure Jimmy will appreciate that."

chapter sixteen

THE TRIP HOME

The boys lost no time in arranging their departure. They were booked on the next PanAm flight out, a late-night departure the following day to New York.

Pan Am landed at 4:03 P.M. Jo and Sandi were the sixth and seventh people off the plane. Jo staggered as the wall of heat hit her. Sandi did not seem to be affected by it at first, but its insidious, relentless attack on her senses finally won the battle.

A new land, new experiences, perhaps the beginning of additional horizons to be mastered, new difficulties to be overcome…all that were aboard the *Alpha II* hoped the lessons learned on this adventure would prove to have a practical application in each one's future.

The flight back to the states was far shorter than the trip across; that was to be expected. What was not expected was the latent reaction each of the boys had - apparently to the pineapple at Tema. Somewhere over mid-Atlantic, the bug hit them, all except Walt. He had apparently exhausted its devastating frenzy in port prior to departure for home, but for the rest of the crew, it was saving its frenzy for the confines of a 707 at about 400 miles per hour. The 707 had five toilets in the rear of the cabin. None of them were large in any sense of the word, and the aircraft had a full passenger load. The boys said later that access to the toilets was

epilogue

FOLLOW YOUR DREAMS

determined by how many of the boys were out of their seats at any one time!

Dreams – the strongest motivating force known to man. Let them guide and direct you. If it weren't for dreams, we would not have had the airplane, the steam engine – so many things we can trace back to a dream. Almost every experience we can call to mind was fostered by a dream of one sort or another – some good, and some great, some contrary, and some disastrous. For every war the world has known was centered in a dream, a dream of conquest, a misplaced dream of superiority.

Even in the Alpha Boat Odyssey, Charley had a dream – a dream of riches, of making much money. That ignited other dreams, dreams that lingered long after the basic dream was realized. For each of the boys, their dreams were of the long term, beneficial variety, filed away in their subconscious minds to be drawn upon when time and seasons demanded. A mini-review of each life illustrates this point:

Rick D. Murray: Graduated from the University of South Florida, was deposed as President, Builders Development and Finance, Inc., in Wayzata, Minnesota, but overcame adiversity to found Residential Development, Inc, in Chanhassen, Minnesota, with projects now in five states including Minnesota, Wisconsin, Missouri, Kansas, and Florida.

Daniel Murray: Graduated from Florida State University, is currently working with and for his brother at RDI as project manager in Kansas and Missouri. He and Debi own a historical building on the square in Liberty, Missouri – the same square where Jesse James staged one of his famous bank robberies.

Walter Murray: Walt was the inventive, compassionate one, graduating from the University of South Florida in Business Administration. Walt felt his calling was in another field, so he elected to pursue Orthodics at the University of Minnesota. He was highly regarded within the medical community at the time of his death in an aircraft accident in.1995. It was a home-built aircraft that he had bought fully assembled from an owner in Atlanta, and had flown it extensively in the eastern states delivering braces that he had fabricated primarily **for** Easter Seals children. It was on such a flight that Walt died on approach to Woodenville Airport, Ohio on May 24, 1995. It was just one of those events that today we will not understand. Some day we may.

James T White: Also a student of Florida State University, Jimmy joined the ranks of the Professional Golfers Association and remains active in Tallahassee, Florida.

Life is made up of choices and their lessons. Choices, in turn are made up of our desires, and our desires are influenced by our experiences, those we have witnessed as well as those in which we have participated. Every choice leaves those who witnessed either elated or depressed, or to languish somewhere between those two extremes. This opportunity led the boys to the threshold of adventure, and the door lay ajar. Their experiences aboard the Alpha Boats left them far stronger in the vagaries of life as well as understanding the fickleness of their fellow man, and that understanding, along with the knowledge of a much greater power than that of mere men, offers the wisdom to overcome every adversity.

What have these adventurers learned from their experience? Many things:

That each possessed an inner strength. There was revealed a side of each neophyte sailor not easily seen except for the experiences they all faced. Their experiences continue to mold and shape the character they have all become, and their rising above each adversity they face has empowered each victor with renewed energy and confidence to face the next challenge with renewed confidence.

They learned to be more tolerant of one another, realizing that a failure on another's part could often be traced to a failure of their own.

They learned to depend upon, and to be depended upon

To establish their goals, and to work to attain them.

That each has limitations, and to appreciate what each can contribute to the benefit of all.

And, above all, they learned that there is a power from above that transcends all other powers, which guides us all in troubled waters.

....

Biblical references from The King James Verson ,Published by The Press Syndicate of the University of Cambridge , Cambridge, UK

Other references; Cmdr Charles Fountain Willis, Jr. off the Internet
And Pegleg Nye, also off the internet.

....

www.ingramcontent.com/pod-product-compliance
Lightning Source LLC
LaVergne TN
LVHW090948080826
845145LV00003B/933

* 9 7 8 1 5 9 9 3 2 0 2 0 5 *